Anonymous

The Proceedings at the Celebration by the Pilgrim Society at Plymouth

The 250th Anniversary of the Landing of the Pilgrims

Anonymous

The Proceedings at the Celebration by the Pilgrim Society at Plymouth
The 250th Anniversary of the Landing of the Pilgrims

ISBN/EAN: 9783337293338

Printed in Europe, USA, Canada, Australia, Japan

Cover: Foto ©Lupo / pixelio.de

More available books at **www.hansebooks.com**

THE

PROCEEDINGS

AT THE

CELEBRATION BY THE PILGRIM SOCIETY

AT PLYMOUTH,

December 21, 1870,

OF THE

Two Hundred and Fiftieth Anniversary

OF THE

LANDING OF THE PILGRIMS.

CAMBRIDGE:
PRESS OF JOHN WILSON AND SON.
1871.

"WE have come to this Rock, to record here our homage for our Pilgrim Fathers; our sympathy in their sufferings; our gratitude for their labors; our admiration of their virtues; our veneration for their piety; and our attachment to those principles of civil and religious liberty, for which they encountered the dangers of the ocean, the storms of heaven, the violence of savages, disease, exile, and famine, to enjoy and establish." — WEBSTER.

INTRODUCTION.

THIS Volume has been prepared, and is now published, in obedience to a vote of the Trustees of the Pilgrim Society passed at a meeting held in the office of the Register of Deeds at Plymouth, on the evening of Friday, December 30, 1870.

At that meeting it was voted that the Vice-President of the Society be requested to prepare and publish the proceedings of the Celebration of the Two Hundred and Fiftieth Anniversary of the Landing of the Pilgrims; and that the Secretary, WILLIAM S. DANFORTH, Esq., be directed to communicate to Hon. ROBERT C. WINTHROP, of Boston, the thanks of the Trustees for the able, eloquent, and instructive oration delivered by him on that occasion, and to request a copy for publication.

PLYMOUTH, January, 1871.

OFFICERS AND TRUSTEES

OF

THE PILGRIM SOCIETY.

President.

HON. EDWARD S. TOBEY . . . . . *ex officio Trustee.*

Vice-President.

HON. WILLIAM T. DAVIS . . . . . *ex officio Trustee.*

Secretary.

WILLIAM S. DANFORTH, ESQ. . . . *ex officio Trustee.*

Treasurer.

ISAAC N. STODDARD, ESQ. . . . . *ex officio Trustee.*

Trustees.

HON. CHARLES G. DAVIS.
  ,, E. C. SHERMAN.
  ,, NATHANIEL B. SHURTLEFF.
  ,, GEORGE S. BOUTWELL.
TIMOTHY GORDON, M.D.
THOMAS LORING, ESQ.
SAMUEL H. DOTEN, ESQ.
CHARLES O. CHURCHILL, ESQ.
GEORGE G. DYER, ESQ.

WILLIAM H. WHITMAN, ESQ.
WILLIAM THOMAS, ESQ.
ABRAHAM JACKSON, ESQ.
JAMES W. SEVER, ESQ.
WILLIAM SAVERY, ESQ.
GEORGE P. HAYWARD, ESQ.
BENJAMIN HATHAWAY, ESQ.
RICHARD WARREN, ESQ.
ELLIS AMES, ESQ.,

Committee of Arrangements.

WILLIAM T. DAVIS, *Chairman.*
E. C. SHERMAN.
WILLIAM H. WHITMAN.
CHARLES G. DAVIS.
WILLIAM S. DANFORTH.
JOHN MORISSEY.

ALBERT MASON.
SAMUEL H. DOTEN.
NATHANIEL BROWN.
RICHARD WARREN, New York.
THOMAS RUSSELL, Boston.
GEORGE P. HAYWARD, Boston.

PRELIMINARY PROCEEDINGS.

AT the annual meeting of the PILGRIM SOCIETY, held at Pilgrim Hall, in Plymouth, at three o'clock, P.M , on Monday, May 30, 1870, it was voted that the Vice-President, together with ISAAC N. STODDARD, Esq., WILLIAM H. WHITMAN, Esq., and Dr. TIMOTHY GORDON, be a Committee to consider the expediency of celebrating the Two Hundred and Fiftieth Anniversary of the Landing of the Pilgrims, occurring on the 21st of December following, and report at an adjourned meeting.[1]

At the adjourned meeting held at the same place on the 14th of June, at three o'clock, P.M., a report of the Committee recommending the Celebration was adopted, and a vote was passed requesting the Trustees to make the necessary arrangements.

At a meeting of the Trustees held at the Plymouth National Bank on the evening of July 5th, at eight o'clock, it was unanimously voted, on motion of RICHARD WARREN, Esq., that a Committee — consisting of the President, Vice-President, and Messrs. GORDON, WARREN, and AMES — wait upon Hon. ROBERT C. WINTHROP, of Boston, and invite him to deliver an Oration before the Society on the 21st of December.[2]

At a meeting of the Trustees held at the same place on the evening of the 7th of September, neither the President nor

Vice-President being present, RICHARD WARREN, Esq., was called to the chair. The Committee appointed to wait on Mr. WINTHROP reported his acceptance of the invitation; and it was then voted that a "Committee of five, of which the Vice-President shall be Chairman, be appointed by the Chairman of the meeting, which shall be a Committee of Arrangements to make preparations for the Celebration, with full power to invite guests, appoint committees, and do all things needful and fitting for the occasion."

The Committee as appointed consisted of—

WILLIAM T. DAVIS, *Chairman*.	WILLIAM H. WHITMAN.
E. C. SHERMAN.	CHARLES G. DAVIS.
WILLIAM S. DANFORTH.	

At a meeting of the Committee of Arrangements held at the house of the Chairman on the evening of September 27th, it was voted to enlarge the Committee by the addition to their number of—

JOHN MORISSEY.	NATHANIEL BROWN.
ALBERT MASON.	RICHARD WARREN, New York.
SAMUEL H. DOTEN.	THOMAS RUSSELL, Boston.
GEORGE P. HAYWARD, Boston.	

It was also voted to invite ALBERT MASON, Esq., to act as Chief Marshal on the day of the Celebration; and WILLIAM S. DANFORTH, Esq., was appointed Treasurer.

[3] It was further voted that a Finance Committee be appointed; and the following gentlemen were selected to act on that Committee:—

GEO. F. WESTON, *Chairman*.	CHARLES C. DOTEN.
E. C. TURNER.	BENJAMIN A. HATHAWAY.
CHARLES H. HOWLAND.	JOHN H. HARLOW.
T. D. SHUMWAY.	CHARLES O. CHURCHILL.
JOHN T. HALL.	L. T. ROBBINS, Jr.
HENRY WHITING, Jr.	RICHARD WARREN, New York.
GEORGE P. HAYWARD, Boston.	

A Committee of Reception was also appointed, consisting of the following gentlemen: —

John Morissey, *Chairman*.	Thomas B. Drew.
Jacob H. Loud.	William H. Nelson.
Thomas Loring.	William Hedge.
Daniel E. Damon.	George F. Andrews.
James Bates.	Charles W. Spooner.
Isaac N. Stoddard.	George G. Dyer.
Jeremiah Farris.	Gideon Perkins.
Elliott Russell.	John J. Russell.

William R. Drew.

It was further voted that the Committee of Arrangements act as a General Committee for the ball, with which it was proposed to close the festivities of the Celebration, and that a board of Honorary Managers be appointed, consisting of the following gentlemen: —

Richard Warren, New York.	J. H. Mitchell, E. Bridgewater.
Thomas Russell, Boston.	William Savery, Carver.
William G. Russell, Boston.	William L. Reed, Abington.
James T. Hayward, Boston.	George W. Wright, Duxbury.
B. W. Harris, Boston.	C. B. H. Fessenden, N. Bedford.
James H. Harlow, Middleboro'.	Charles F. Swift, Yarmouth.

The following gentlemen were selected as Floor Managers of the ball: —

Henry G. Parker, Boston.	William P. Stoddard.
Dwight Faulkner.	James D. Thurber.
Francis H. Russell.	Henry W. Loring.
B. M. Watson, Jr.	Robert B. Churchill.
Benjamin O. Strong.	Edward W. Russell, New York.

Isaac Damon, Bridgewater.

At subsequent meetings of the Committee of Arrangements, it was voted to have a public dinner in the new railway passenger station, the use of which the officers of the Old Colony and Newport Railway Company had kindly tendered to the Committee; and a contract was concluded with Mr. L. E. Field, of Taunton, to furnish the dinner, and also the supper for the ball. The Standish Guards, of Plymouth, were invited to perform escort duty, and to be the guests of the Society at the dinner on the day of the Celebration. Gilmore's Band, of Boston, and the Plymouth Brass Band were engaged for the occasion, and every step was taken on a liberal scale to insure a commemoration worthy of the day and creditable to the town.

By a vote of the Committee, the following clergymen were invited to conduct the services in the church : —

Rev. R. H. NEALE, D.D., Boston.
Rev. F. H. HEDGE, D.D., Brookline.
Rev. J. A. M. CHAPMAN, Boston.
Rev. J. P. THOMPSON, D. D., New York.
Rev. T. E. ST. JOHN, Worcester.
Rev. F. N. KNAPP, Plymouth.

Letters of invitation to be present at the Celebration as guests of the Society were sent to the following gentlemen : —

His Excellency ULYSSES S. GRANT . . *President of the United States.*
Hon. SCHUYLER COLFAX . . . *Vice-President of the United States.*
„ HAMILTON FISH . . . . *Secretary of State.*
„ J. C. B. DAVIS . . . . . . *Assistant Secretary of State.*
„ GEORGE S. BOUTWELL . . . . . *Secretary of the Treasury.*
„ WILLIAM A. RICHARDSON . *Assistant Secretary of the Treasury.*
„ COLUMBUS DELANO . . . . . . *Secretary of the Interior.*
„ WILLIAM W. BELKNAP . . . . *Secretary of War.*
„ G. M. ROBESON . . . . *Secretary of the Navy.*
„ J. A. J. CRESSWELL . . . . *Postmaster-General.*
„ AMOS T. AKERMAN . . . . *Attorney-General.*
„ NATHAN CLIFFORD . *Associate Justice Supreme Court of U. S.*
Gen. WILLIAM T. SHERMAN . . . . *Washington.*
Maj.-Gen. O. O. HOWARD . . . . „
„ JOHN M. CORSE . . . . „
Hon. EDWARD THORNTON . . . . *British Minister.*
„ J. W. PATTERSON . . . . *United States Senate.*
„ MATT. H. CARPENTER . . . . . „ „
„ HANNIBAL HAMLIN . . . . „ „
„ JAMES W. NYE . . . . . . „ „
„ CHARLES SUMNER . . . . . . „ „
„ HENRY WILSON . . . . . „ „

Hon. JAMES A. GARFIELD	United States House of Representatives.	
„ WILLIAM D. KELLY	„ „ „	
„ JAMES BUFFINTON	„ „ „	
„ B. F. BUTLER	„ „ „	
„ OAKES AMES	„ „ „	
„ GENERY TWICHELL	„ „ „	
„ SAMUEL HOOPER	„ „ „	
„ NATHANIEL P. BANKS	„ „ „	
„ GEORGE M. BROOKS	„ „ „	
„ GEORGE F. HOAR	„ „ „	
„ HENRY L. DAWES	„ „ „	
„ WILLIAM B. WASHBURNE	„ „ „	
„ CALEB CUSHING	Washington.	
„ GEORGE BANCROFT	Berlin.	
„ J. L. MOTLEY	London.	
„ GEORGE P. MARSH	Turin.	
Commodore JAMES ALDEN	Washington.	
Hon. JOSHUA L. CHAMBERLIN	Governor of Maine.	
„ ONSLOW STEARNS	Governor of New Hampshire.	
„ JOHN W. STEWARD	Governor of Vermont.	
„ SETH PADELFORD	Governor of Rhode Island.	
„ JAMES E. ENGLISH	Governor of Connecticut.	
„ CHARLES S. BRADLEY	Late Chief Justice of Rhode Island.	
„ MORTON MCMICHAEL	Philadelphia.	
JAY COOKE, Esq.	Philadelphia.	
Hon. HORACE GREELEY	Ex-Member of Congress, New York.	
„ JOSEPH H. CHOATE	President N. E. Society of New York.	
„ WILLIAM M. EVARTS	New York, Ex-Attorney-General U. S.	
RICHARD WARREN, Esq.	New York, Ex-President Pilgrim Society.	
GEORGE W. CURTIS, Esq.	New York.	
WILLIAM C. BRYANT, Esq.	„	
Rev. HENRY W. BELLOWS, D.D.	„	
President T. D. WOLSEY	Yale College.	
President CHARLES W. ELIOT	Harvard College.	
Rev. HENRY WARD BEECHER, D.D.	Brooklyn, N. Y.	
Rev. RICHARD S. STORRS, Jr., D.D.	Brooklyn, N. Y.	
SAMUEL COPP BREWSTER, Esq.	Syracuse, N. Y.	
C. B. DOTY, Esq.	Steubenville, Ohio.	
Hon. T. STERRY HUNT	President N. E. Society in Montreal.	
„ GEORGE PARTRIDGE	President N. E. Society in St. Louis.	
Hon. GEORGE T. DAVIS	Portland, Ex-Member of Congress.	

His Excellency WILLIAM CLAFLIN . . . *Governor of Massachusetts.*
Colonel A. B. UNDERWOOD . . . ⎫
   „   JAMES L. BATES . . . . ⎬ *Aids to the Governor of Massa-*
   „   EDWARD N. HALLOWELL . ⎨   *chusetts.*
   „   CHARLES F. WALCOTT . . ⎭
His Honor JOSEPH TUCKER . *Lieutenant-Governor of Massachusetts.*
Hon. WILLIAM L. REED . . . . . . *Of the Executive Council.*
   „   CHARLES ADAMS, Jr. . . . . „   „   „
   „   M. S. UNDERWOOD . . . . „   „   „
   „   R. G. USHER . . . . „   „   „
   „   WILLIAM WINN . . . . „   „   „
   „   H. G. CROWELL . . . . „   „   „
   „   SYLVANDER JOHNSON . . . . . . „   „   „
   „   PETER HARVEY . . . . „   „   „
   „   OLIVER WARNER . . . *Secretary of the Commonwealth.*
   „   JACOB H. LOUD . . . . *Treasurer and Receiver-General.*
   „   CHARLES ENDICOTT . . . . *Auditor.*
   „   Hon. STEPHEN N. GIFFORD . . . . *Clerk of Mass. Senate.*
Maj.-Gen. JAMES A. CUNNINGHAM . . . *Adjutant-General of Mass.*
Hon. REUBEN A. CHAPMAN . *Chief Justice Supreme Court of Mass.*
   „   L. F. BRIGHAM . . . *Chief Justice Superior Court of Mass.*
   „   CHARLES ALLEN . . . . *Attorney-General of Massachusetts.*
   „   HORACE H. COOLEDGE . . . *President of Massachusetts Senate.*
   „   HARVEY JEWELL . . . *Speaker Mass. House of Representatives.*
   „   CHARLES F. ADAMS . . . . *Boston, Late Minister to England.*
   „   CHARLES H. WARREN . *Ex-President of the Pilgrim Society.*
   „   JOHN H. CLIFFORD . . . *New Bedford, Ex-Governor of Mass.*
   „   ALEXANDER H. BULLOCK . . *Worcester, Ex-Governor of Mass.*
Prof. HENRY W. LONGFELLOW . . . . *Harvard College.*
   „   JAMES RUSSELL LOWELL . . . . . .   „   „
WILLIAM EVERETT, Esq. . . . .   „   „
Hon. GEORGE S. HILLARD . . . . *United States Attorney.*
   „   THOMAS RUSSELL . . . . *Collector of Boston.*
   „   JOHN G. WHITTIER . . . . *Amesbury.*
   „   E. ROCKWOOD HOAR *Concord, Late Attorney-General U. S.*
   „   CHARLES W. UPHAM . . *Salem, Ex-Member of Congress.*
   „   JOHN G. PALFREY . *Cambridge, Ex-Member of Congress.*
   „   GEORGE B. LORING . . . . *Salem.*
   „   WALTER S. HARRIMAN . . . *Ex-Governor of New Hampshire.*
   „   NATHANIEL B. SHURTLEFF . . . . *Mayor of Boston.*
   „   GEORGE W. WARREN   *Charlestown, President Bunker Hill*
                                        Monument Association.

Hon. GEORGE MARSTON . . . . *New Bedford.*
" WILLIAM H. WOOD . . . . *Middleboro'.*
" WILLIAM S. CLARK . *Amherst, Pres. Mass. Agricultural College.*
" ARTEMAS HALE . . . . *Bridgewater, Ex-Member of Congress.*
" BENJAMIN HOBART . *Abington, oldest living Graduate Brown University.*
WILLIAM L. GARRISON, Esq. . . . . *Boston.*
WILLIAM H. BULLOCK, Esq. . . . . "
HAMMATT BILLINGS, Esq. . . *Boston, Architect of the National Monument to the Pilgrims.*
OLIVER W. HOLMES, M.D. . . . . *Boston.*
Rev. EDWARD E. HALE . . . . "
Capt. R. A. FENGAR . . . . *United States Revenue Service.*
S. B. NOYES, Esq. . . . . *Canton.*
Rev. EDWARD N. KIRK . . . . *Boston.*
" J. M. MANNING . . . . "
" EDWARDS A. PARK . . . . *Andover.*
" EDMUND H. SEARS . . . . *Weston.*
" JOSEPH RICHARDSON . . . . *Hingham.*

The following Associations were also invited to send delegates to attend the Celebration and be the guests of the Pilgrim Society : —

Massachusetts Historical Society . . . . *Boston.*
American Antiquarian Society . . . . . . *Worcester.*
New England Historic-Genealogical Society . . . *Boston.*
Historical Society of Connecticut . . . . . . *New Haven.*
New York Historical Society . . . . *New York.*
Cape Cod Association . . . .
New England Society . . . . . . *Cincinnati.*
" " . . . . *New York.*
" " . . . . *Chicago.*
" " . . . . . . *Montreal.*
" " . . . . . . *New Orleans.*
" " . . . . . . *St. Louis.*
" " . . . . . . *San Francisco.*
" " . . . . . . *Aurora, Nevada.*

The day of the Celebration was such as is rarely seen in winter. The ground was free from both snow and frost, the sky cloudless, and the air as mild as that of early November.

During the early hours of the morning the streets of Plymouth were enlivened by numerous arrivals from the neighboring towns; and at ten o'clock a special express train of eleven cars arrived from Boston, bringing most of the invited guests and a large number of visitors. At eleven o'clock the regular train arrived with larger numbers, and all were warmly welcomed to the hospitalities of the town. To avoid the difficulty of discovering the invited guests at the station on the arrival of the trains, and extricating them from the crowd, the Committee of Reception had delegated two of their number to go to Boston, and return in the cars with the guests, and present them to their Chairman on their arrival. They were at once taken in carriages to the house of the Chairman of the Committee of Arrangements, who held a public reception, and from there escorted to the Court House, from whence they were to take carriages for the procession. On the arrival of the regular train at eleven o'clock, the members of the Pilgrim Society, and citizens intending to join the procession to the church where the services were to be held, met at Pilgrim Hall. At a quarter past eleven, the Chief Marshal Captain ALBERT MASON, with his aids Captains CHARLES C. DOTEN and JAMES D. THURBER, and his assistants —

Capt. JOSIAH C. FULLER,	BENJAMIN A. HATHAWAY,
,, CHARLES B. STODDARD,	JOSEPH L. WESTON,
GEORGE F. ANDREWS,	CHANDLER HOLMES,
JAMES M. ATWOOD,	THOMAS D. SHUMWAY,
WILLIAM HEDGE,	GEORGE H. JACKSON, and
CHARLES H. HOWLAND,	JOHN H. HARLOW,

with the exception of those detailed for duty at the church, formed the procession; which soon after moved in the following order through Court, North, Water, and Leyden Streets, to the Church of the First Parish : —

PRELIMINARY PROCEEDINGS. 15

Escort.
The Standish Guards, Captain JOSIAH R. DREW,
Accompanied by the Plymouth Brass Band.
Aid. Chief Marshal. Aid.
The Hon. EDWARD S. TOBEY, President of the Society.
The Hon. WILLIAM T. DAVIS, Vice-President of the Society.
The Hon. ROBERT C. WINTHROP, the Orator of the Day,
And the invited guests, as follows: —

Hon. Henry Wilson.
,, Charles F. Adams.
,, Onslow Stearns.
,, John H. Clifford.
,, George S. Hillard.
,, Charles S. Bradley.
,, Nathaniel B. Shurtleff.
,, Thomas Russell.
,, George T. Davis.
,, George W. Warren.
,, Artemas Hale.
,, Benjamin Hobart.
,, Charles Endicott.
,, Walter S. Harriman.
,, Jacob H. Loud.
,, Stephen N. Gifford.
,, Emory Washburn, Delegate of Mass Hist. Soc

Hon. Stephen Salisbury, Delegate of Amer. Antiquarian Soc.
,, Marshal P. Wilder, Delegate of New Eng. Hist. Gen. Soc.
,, T. Sterry Hunt.
Rev. Frederick H. Hedge, D.D.
,, Rollin H. Neale, D.D.
,, Joseph P. Thompson, D.D.
,, J. A. M. Chapman.
,, T. E. St. John.
,, Frederick N. Knapp.
Gen. O. O. Howard.
Mr. William Everett.
,, Samuel B. Noyes.
,, Hammatt Billings.
Capt. R. A. Fengar.
Col. A. B. Underwood.
,, Charles F. Walcott.

Committee of Arrangements and Committee of Reception.
Gilmore's Band, of Boston.
Officers and Trustees of the Pilgrim Society.
Members of the Pilgrim Society.
Other Organizations, and Citizens.

As the procession passed the Rock, a national salute was fired on board the United States Revenue Steamer "Mahoning," anchored in the harbor; a courtesy for which the Committee were indebted to the Commander of the Cutter, Captain R. A. FENGAR, who was one of the guests of the Society.

The church had been opened for the admission of ladies to reserved seats at a quarter past eleven o'clock; and on the arrival of the procession it was at once filled to its utmost capacity. Gilmore's Band was stationed in the gallery, together with a double quartette choir, composed of the following singers: soprano, Mrs. Winslow B. Standish and Miss Olive Collingwood; contralto, Mrs. E. B. Atwood and Miss Lena Rich; tenor, Messrs. Joseph L. Brown and John H. Harlow; basso, Messrs. Charles H. Richardson and James M. Atwood. Seats and tables for members of the Press were arranged in the cross-aisle in front of the pulpit; and the following journals were represented: —

Old Colony Memorial and Plymouth Rock	*Plymouth.*
Old Colony Sentinel	,,
Abington Standard	*Abington.*
Hingham Journal	*Hingham.*
North Bridgewater Gazette	*North Bridgewater.*
Middleboro' Gazette	*Middleboro'.*
New Bedford Standard	*New Bedford.*
Weymouth Gazette	*Weymouth.*
Yarmouth Register	*Yarmouth Port.*
Daily Advertiser	*Boston.*
Boston Journal	,,
Evening Traveller	,,
Boston Herald	,,
Boston Post	,,
Evening Transcript	,,
Suffolk County Journal	,,
Commercial Bulletin	,,
Saturday Evening Gazette	,,
Free Press	*Northampton.*
Hartford Courant	*Hartford.*
Advance	*Chicago.*
Christian Union	*New York.*
Evening Post	,,
Independent	,,
Mexico Independent	*Mexico, N. Y.*

At a quarter past twelve the services commenced.

Services in the Church.

I.

VOLUNTARY.

Prayer from "Moses in Egypt," by Gilmore's Band.

II.

ODE.

Composed by Hon. JOHN DAVIS, for the Celebration in 1792; read by Rev. ROLLIN H. NEALE, D.D., of Boston; and sung by the Choir to the tune of "America," with Orchestral Accompaniment.

    SONS of renowned sires,
    Join in harmonious choirs,
        Swell your loud songs;
    Daughters of peerless dames,
    Come with your mild acclaims,
    Let their revered names
        Dwell on your tongues.

    From frowning Albion's seat
    See the famed band retreat,
        On ocean tost;
    Blue tumbling billows roar,
    By keel scarce ploughed before,
    And bear them to this shore
        Fettered with frost.

    By yon wave-beaten rock
    See the illustrious flock
        Collected stand;

To seek some sheltering grove
Their faithful partners move,
Dear pledges of their love
    In either hand.

Not winter's sullen face,
Not the fierce tawny race
    In arms arrayed,
Not hunger, shook their faith;
Not sickness' baleful breath
Nor Carver's early death
    Their souls dismayed.

Watered by heavenly dew,
The germ of Empire grew,
    Freedom its root;
From the cold northern pine,
Far tow'rd the burning line,
Spreads the luxuriant vine,
    Bending with fruit.

Columbia, child of Heaven!
The best of blessings given
    Be thine to greet;
Hailing this votive day,
Looking with fond survey
Upon the weary way
    Of Pilgrim feet.

Here trace the moss-grown stones
Where rest their mould'ring bones,
    Again to rise;
And let thy sons be led
To emulate the dead,
While o'er their tombs they tread
    With moisten'd eyes.

III.

READING

Of the following Selections from the Scriptures, by Rev. FREDERIC H. HEDGE, D.D., of Brookline, Mass.

Psalm CXXIV.

IF it had not been the Lord who was on our side, now may Israel say;

2 If it had not been the Lord who was on our side, when men rose up against us:

3 Then they had swallowed us up quick, when their wrath was kindled against us:

4 Then the waters had overwhelmed us, the stream had gone over our soul:

5 Then the proud waters had gone over our soul.

6 Blessed be the Lord, who hath not given us as a prey to their teeth.

7 Our soul is escaped as a bird out of the snare of the fowlers: the snare is broken, and we are escaped.

8 Our help is in the name of the Lord, who made heaven and earth.

Genesis XII.

1 Now the Lord had said unto Abram, Get thee out of thy country, and from thy kindred, and from thy father's house, unto a land that I will shew thee:

2 And I will make of thee a great nation, and I will bless thee, and make thy name great; and thou shalt be a blessing:

3 And I will bless them that bless thee, and curse him that curseth thee: and in thee shall all families of the earth be blessed.

Hebrews XI.

1 Now faith is the substance of things hoped for, the evidence of things not seen.

2 For by it the elders obtained a good report.

8 By faith Abraham, when he was called to go out into a place which he should after receive for an inheritance, obeyed; and he went out, not knowing whither he went.

9 By faith he sojourned in the land of promise, as in a strange country, dwelling in tabernacles with Isaac and Jacob, the heirs with him of the same promise:

10 For he looked for a city which hath foundations, whose builder and maker is God.

12 Therefore sprang there even of one, and him as good as dead, so many as the stars of the sky in multitude, and as the sand which is by the sea shore innumerable.

13 These all died in faith, not having received the promises, but having seen them afar off, and were persuaded of them, and embraced them, and confessed that they were strangers and pilgrims on the earth.

14 For they that say such things declare plainly that they seek a country.

15 And truly, if they had been mindful of that country, from whence they came out, they might have had opportunity to have returned.

16 But now they desire a better country, that is, an heavenly: wherefore God is not ashamed to be called their God: for he hath prepared for them a city.

39 And these all, having obtained a good report through faith, received not the promise:

40 God having provided some better thing for us, that they without us should not be made perfect.

Psalm CVII.

1 O give thanks unto the Lord, for he is good: for his mercy endureth for ever.

2 Let the redeemed of the Lord say so, whom he hath redeemed from the hand of the enemy;

3 And gathered them out of the lands, from the east, and from the west, from the north, and from the south.

4 They wandered in the wilderness in a solitary way; they found no city to dwell in.

5 Hungry and thirsty, their soul fainted in them.

6 Then they cried unto the Lord in their trouble, and he delivered them out of their distresses.

7 And he led them forth by the right way, that they might go to a city of habitation.

8 Oh that men would praise the Lord for his goodness, and for his wonderful works to the children of men!

9 For he satisfieth the longing soul, and filleth the hungry soul with goodness.

32 Let them exalt him also in the congregation of the people, and praise him in the assembly of the elders.

33 He turneth rivers into a wilderness, and the water-springs into dry ground;

34 A fruitful land into barrenness, for the wickedness of them that dwell therein.

35 He turneth the wilderness into a standing water, and dry ground into water-springs.

36 And there he maketh the hungry to dwell, that they may prepare a city for habitation;

37 And sow the fields, and plant vineyards, which may yield fruits of increase.

40 He poureth contempt upon princes, and causeth them to wander in the wilderness, where there is no way.

41 Yet setteth he the poor on high from affliction, and maketh him families like a flock.

42 The righteous shall see it, and rejoice: and all iniquity shall stop her mouth.

43 Whoso is wise, and will observe these things, even they shall understand the loving-kindness of the Lord.

MATTHEW VII.

16 Ye shall know them by their fruits: do men gather grapes of thorns, or figs of thistles?

17 Even so every good tree bringeth forth good fruit; but a corrupt tree bringeth forth evil fruit.

18 A good tree cannot bring forth evil fruit, neither can a corrupt tree bring forth good fruit.

19 Every tree that bringeth not forth good fruit is hewn down, and cast into the fire.

20 Wherefore, by their fruits ye shall know them.

21 Not every one that saith unto me, Lord, Lord, shall enter into the kingdom of heaven, but he that doeth the will of my Father which is in heaven.

22 Many will say to me in that day, Lord, Lord, have we not prophesied in thy name? and in thy name have cast out devils? and in thy name done many wonderful works?

23 And then will I profess unto them, I never knew you: depart from me, ye that work iniquity.

24 Therefore, whosoever heareth these sayings of mine, and doeth them, I will liken him unto a wise man, which built his house upon a rock:

25 And the rain descended, and the floods came, and the winds blew, and beat upon that house; and it fell not: for it was founded upon a rock.

26 And every one that heareth these sayings of mine, and doeth them not, shall be likened unto a foolish man, which built his house upon the sand:

27 And the rain descended, and the floods came, and the winds blew, and beat upon that house; and it fell: and great was the fall of it.

IV.

HYMN.

Composed for the occasion by Hon. WILLIAM T. DAVIS; read by Rev. J. A. M. CHAPMAN, of Boston; and sung by the Choir, with Orchestral Accompaniment, to a tune composed for the occasion by C. A. WHITE, of Boston.[6]

> To Thee, O God! whose guiding hand
> Our Fathers led across the sea,
> And brought them to this barren shore,
> Where they might freely worship Thee;
>
> To Thee, O God! whose arm sustained
> Their footsteps in this desert land,
> Where sickness lurked and death assailed,
> And foes beset on every hand;
>
> To Thee, O God! we lift our eyes;
> To Thee our grateful voices raise,
> And, kneeling at Thy gracious throne,
> Devoutly join in hymns of praise.
>
> Our Fathers' God! incline Thine ear,
> And listen to our heartfelt prayer;
> Surround us with Thy heavenly grace,
> And guard us with Thy constant care.
>
> Our Fathers' God! in Thee *we'll* trust;
> Sheltered by Thee from every harm,
> *We'll* follow where Thy hand shall guide,
> And lean on Thy sustaining arm.

V.

ORATION.

By Hon. ROBERT C. WINTHROP, of Boston.

THERE can be no true New England heart which does not throb to-day with something of unwonted exultation. There can be no true American heart, I think, which has not found itself swelling with a more fervent gratitude to God, and a more profound veneration for the Pilgrim Fathers, as this morning's sun has risen above the hill-tops, in an almost midsummer glory, and ushered in, once more, with such transcendent splendor, our consecrated Jubilee.

When we reflect on the influence which has flowed, and is still flowing, in ever fresh and ceaseless streams, from yonder Rock, which two centuries and a half ago was struck for the first time by the foot of civilized, Christian man; when we reflect how mightily that influence has prevailed, and how widely it has pervaded the world, — inspiring and aiding the settlement of Massachusetts, and, through Massachusetts, of all New England, and, through New England, of so large a part of our whole widespread country, and thus, through the example of our country and its institutions, extending the principles of civil and religious freedom to the remotest regions of the earth, leaving no corner of Christendom, or even of Heathendom, unvisited or unrefreshed, — we should be dead, indeed, to every emotion of gratitude to God or man, were we not to hail this Anniversary as one of the grandest in the calendar of the ages.

We are here, my friends, to celebrate the Fifth Jubilee of what is now known emphatically, whereever the history of New England, or the history of America, is read, as "The Landing." No other landing, temporary or permanent, upon our own or upon any other shore, can ever usurp its title, or ever supersede or weaken its hold upon the world's remembrance and regard.

There have been other landings, I need hardly say, which have left a proud and shining mark on the historic page: Landings of discoverers; landings of conquerors; landings of kings or princes, called by right of restoration or revolution to take possession of time-honored thrones ; landings of organized Colonies, from large and well-appointed fleets, on conspicuous coasts, to occupy territories opened and prepared, in some degree, for human habitation.

Not such was the landing which we commemorate to-day. Not such the event which has rendered this shortest day of all the year so memorable for ever in the annals of human freedom. It was the landing of a few weary and wave-worn men from a single ship, — nay, from a single shallop, —

on a bleak and desolate shore, amid the storms and tempests of a well-nigh arctic winter, with none to welcome, none even to witness it. I might, indeed, be almost pardoned for saying, that the sun itself stood still in the heavens to behold it! But there were, certainly, no other witnesses, save those witnesses to each other's constancy and courage who were themselves the actors in the scene, and that all-seeing, omnipresent God, who guided and guarded all their steps.

Turn back with me to that epoch of the winter solstice, just two hundred and fifty years ago, and let us spend at least a portion of this flying hour in attempting to recall the precise incidents which then occurred on the spot on which we are assembled, with some of their immediate antecedents and consequences. There have been, and will be, other occasions for boasting, if any one desires to boast, of what New England has accomplished, directly or indirectly, for herself or for mankind, in later times. There have been, and will be, other opportunities for a general glorification of New England principles, New England achievements, New England inventions and discoveries, past or present, remote or recent. We recognize them all to-day, — all, at least, that are worthy of being recognized at all, — as the legitimate result and development of this day's doings. We count and claim the progress of our country, in its best and worthiest sense, as the

"Pilgrims' Progress;" — as the grand and glorious advance upon a line of march in which they were the pioneers, and for which they, in their own expressive phrase, literally as well as metaphorically, were the instruments "to break the ice for others."

To them the honors of this day are due. To their memories this Anniversary is sacred. Once in fifty years, certainly, we may well refresh our remembrance of what they did and suffered, and still more of the aims and ends of all their doings and sufferings. It is an old story, it is true; but there are some old stories which are almost forgotten into newness. There are some old stories which are actually new to every rising generation, and of whose real interest and nobleness thousands of young hearts receive their first vivid impression from what may be said or done on some occasion like the present. There are some old stories, too, of which even those who hold them in fondest and most familiar remembrance are never weary; and the appetite for which no repetitions can ever cloy, or even satisfy. There are some old stories, let me add, — and this is eminently one of them, — around which a haze, or it may be a halo, of legend and romance is gradually allowed to gather and thicken with the lapse of years, and which require and demand to be set forth afresh, from time to time, in their true simplicity and grandeur.

But there is no longer an excuse for doubt or uncertainty as to any substantial statement relating to the Pilgrim Fathers. Tradition, legend, romance, can find "no jutty, frieze, buttress, nor coigne of vantage, for their pendent bed and procreant cradle," in that solid structure of fact and truth which has recently been built up, — let me rather say, which has recently been discovered and unveiled, in all the simple beauty of its original proportions, — by the loving students and diligent investigators of Pilgrim history.

It is, indeed, a peculiar advantage of all young countries like our own, that, originating in a period of written and printed records, they may trace back the current of their career to its primal source and spring, without leaving room for any intermixture of myth or fable. Yet written or even printed records may disappear, or be overlooked and forgotten for a time, — awaiting such a search and such a scrutiny as Grote and Niebuhr, and Merivale and Mommsen, have recently brought to the history of Greece or Rome ; or as Froude, even more remarkably, has just given to the history of England's Queen Elizabeth.

Even such a search and such a scrutiny have of late been applied to the history of the little band whose landing we are here to commemorate, and most richly have they been rewarded. Since the last Jubilee of the Pilgrims was celebrated, fifty years ago, — when that grand discourse of New England's grandest orator and statesman summoned the attention of the world so emphatically to their sublime but simple story, — antiquarians at home and abroad, pious and painstaking students, American travellers in foreign lands not forgetful of their own, one and all, have seemed inflamed with a new zeal to subject that story to the closest examination; to sift out from it everything conjectural and legendary; and to investigate the Pilgrim track, footstep by footstep, wherever it could be found, in the Old World as well as in the New. Nothing has been too minute or trivial to elude their search; nothing too seemingly inscrutable to repel or discourage their pursuit; nothing too generally credited to satisfy their eagerness for positive proof and authentic verification. As the marvellous growth of that majestic perennial, of which the Mayflower supplied the seed, has been developed and displayed, with all its myriad leaves for the healing of the nations, and all its magic branches for sweetening so many bitter fountains, and all its rich and varied fruits for ourselves and for mankind, they have been more and more incited to trace back that seed to its native bed; to analyze with almost chemical exactness its smallest seminal principles; and to ascertain precisely by what culture, and by what hands, it was made so to take root upon a rock, and to bud and blossom and bear so abundantly in a wilderness.

We owe these laborious investigators a deep debt of gratitude, and it is fit that we should not forget them, this day, as we avail ourselves of their researches. I need but name the late admirable Judge Davis, whose excellent edition of " Morton's Memorial " led the way in the later illustrations of Pilgrim history. I need but name the late Reverend Dr. Alexander Young, whose "Chronicles of Plymouth" ought to be fresh in the memory of every son and daughter of the old Colony. But let me recall more deliberately a venerable antiquary of Old England, whom it was my good fortune to meet at the breakfast-table of the celebrated historian Hallam, nearly a quarter of a century ago, — the late Reverend Joseph Hunter; who, having diversified his routine of service, in her Majesty's Public Record Office, by tracts illustrative of the great triumphs of his own country in arms and in literature, — triumphs by the sword of Henry V. at Agincourt, and triumphs by the pens of Shakspeare and Milton in the fields of epic or dramatic poetry, — turned to the Pilgrims of Plymouth, and to the Puritans of Massachusetts, for the latest and best themes of his unwearied investigations. To him we primarily owe it that we can follow back that little band, to which the name of Brownists had been contemptuously given, to the very hive from which they first swarmed, — that little circle in Yorkshire and Nottinghamshire, and not far from Lincolnshire, around which he so fitly inscribed the legend, "Maximæ gentis incunabula," — the cradle of the greatest nation. By the light of his antiquarian torch we are able to fix the precise locality and surroundings of the old Manor Place of Scrooby, — formerly a palace of the Archbishops of York, and which had often been the residence of at least one of them, "that he might enjoy the diversion of hunting" in the neighboring chase of Hatfield; which was occupied as a refuge for many weeks by the great lord Cardinal Wolsey, when, having "ventured in a sea of glory, but far beyond his depth," he had at last been left, "weary and old with service, to the mercy of a rude stream," which was for ever to hide him; and which, not many years afterwards, Henry the Eighth himself had selected for a resting-place, during one of his Royal progresses to the north; — but which, half a century later, had become the home of one, whose occupation of it, even for an hour, would have given it a celebrity and a sanctity in our remembrance and regard, which neither Archbishops, nor Cardinals, nor Kings, could have imparted to it in a lifetime.

There, in that "manor of the Bishops," of which, alas! hardly a fragment is now left, lived WILLIAM BREWSTER, — one of the noblest of the men whom we are here to commemorate, and not unworthy to be named first of all, on such an occasion as this. Educated at the University of Cambridge, and having served as the faithful Secretary of the accomplished Davison (Queen Elizabeth's Ambassador in Holland, and afterwards one of her Secretaries of State), — until Davison's too prompt and implicit obedience to the orders of his Royal Mistress in the matter of poor Mary, Queen of Scots, had afforded a pretext for discarding him, — Brewster had retired with disgust from the pomps and vanities, the caprices and cruelties, of the Court, and had given himself up to religious meditation and study. Deeply impressed with the corruptions and superstitions, the prelatical assumptions and tyrannies, of the English Church, as it then existed, in those earlier transition stages of the Reformation, he had united himself with one of the little bodies of Separatists from that communion, and soon became " a special help and stay to them." At his house, — this very "manor of the Bishops," which Mr. Hunter helped us to identify, — we learn that the members of the church of which the sainted Robinson was the pastor, the church of our Plymouth Pilgrims, "ordinarily met on the Lord's Day; and with great love he entertained them when they came, making provision for them to his great charge; and continued so to do while they could stay in England."

Our mother country has many spots within her dominions which are dear to the hearts of the lovers of religious and of civil liberty in both hemispheres: The plain of Runnymede, the Lollard's Tower, the

Tower of London, the Martyrs' Monument at Oxford, the glorious Abbey of Westminster, the grand Cathedrals in almost every county; but I know of none more worthy of being visited with pious reverence, by every American traveller certainly, than that old original site of Brewster's residence in Nottinghamshire; nor one which more deserves to be marked, not indeed by any ostentatious or sumptuous structure, out of all keeping with the plain and frugal character of those who have made it memorable for ever, but by some appropriate monument, a chapel or a school-house, erected by the care and at the cost of the sons and daughters of New England. We all remember that John Cotton's chapel at Old Boston was restored, not many years ago, by the contributions of a few of the generous sons of New Boston. The place where Robinson and Brewster gathered that first Pilgrim Church is certainly not less worthy of commemoration.

But it is not only the residence of Brewster which the researches of good Mr. Hunter, the very Nimrod of Antiquaries, have revealed to us. There, within that charmed circle — the cradle of the greatest nation — he helped us to discover a birthplace, which owing to a blundering misprint had so long baffled the most eager search; the birthplace of one who might almost contest with Brewster himself the right to be named first at any commemoration of the Pilgrim Fathers, — their Governor for thirty years, their Historian, their principal writer both in prose and verse, and second to no one of them, from first to last, in the fidelity and devotion with which he sustained and illustrated their principles. There, within that same charmed circle, of which the little market town of Bawtry is the centre, and the greater part, if not the whole, of which is now the property of one whose recent title, as a peer, has not obliterated our remembrance of his name as a poet, and who may be recalled with the more pleasure at this hour as one of the few among the English nobility who sympathized with the North in our late war for the Union, — there, in the record book of the little church of Austerfield, still standing, has been found the distinct entry, "William, son of William, Bradfourth, baptized the XIXth day of March, Anno Dñi 1589."

I hold in my hand a photographic picture of that ancient edifice, and one, too, of the registered entry of Bradford's baptism, given me two or three years ago by Lord Houghton, — Monckton Milnes that was, — now Lord of the Manor, I believe, — and which I would gladly deposit in your Pilgrim Museum, if they are not there already.

The font from which Bradford was christened, and the altar-rails at which his parents doubtless kneeled — for he must have been baptized according to the rites, and by a pastor of the Church of England — are still preserved. But neither pastor nor parents could have dreamed, as the infant boy winced, perhaps, from the coldness of that sprinkled water, and shrunk, it may be, from the signing with the sign of the cross upon his tiny forehead, how sturdy and uncompromising a hater he was to become, in his mature life, of all mere forms and shows and ceremonies of religion; and, at the same time, how earnest and ardent and devoted a lover and upholder of the great truths and doctrines of which these were but the outward and visible signs.

Bradford and Brewster, if I mistake not, are the only two of our Pilgrim leaders, who can be distinctly identified with that little church at Scrooby, of which the venerable Richard Clifton and the zealous John Robinson were the associated pastor and teacher, and out of which came this first permanent settlement of New England. Bradford, indeed, was but a boy in age, at that early period, — hardly more than sixteen years old, an orphan boy, — and must have been like a son to Brewster, who was thirty years his senior; but he was a boy who seems to have known " little more of the state of childhood but its innocency and pleasantness," and who was capable, even then, of rendering no feeble aid and comfort to his maturer leader and friend. Together they braved persecution. Together they bore the taunts and scoffs of neighbors and relatives. Together they embraced exile. Together they were cast into prison at old Boston in Lincolnshire.

Together, after a brief separation, — for Bradford was liberated first on account of his youth, — they found refuge in Holland. Together they embarked in the Mayflower. Together they were associated for three and twenty years, — for Brewster lived in a vigorous old age till 1643, — in establishing and ruling the Pilgrim plantation here at New Plymouth.

Brewster and Bradford, the Æneas and Ascanius of our grand Pilgrim Epic, — I might better have said, the Paul and Timothy, or be it Titus, of our New England, Plymouth, Separatist Church, — both of them laymen, but both of them, by life and word, by precept and example, showing forth the great doctrines of Christ, their Saviour, with a power and a persuasiveness which might well have been envied by any pastor or preacher or lordly prelate of that or any other day: — For ever honored be their names in New England history and in New England hearts! Alas! that no portrait of either of them is left, — if, indeed, in their simplicity and modesty, they would ever have allowed one to be taken, — so that their image, as well as their names and their example, might be held up to the contemplation of our country and of mankind for endless generations!

But the little church of which they were members was able, as we know, to maintain its precarious and perilous existence at Scrooby, for hardly more than a single year, certainly for not more than two years. It could find indeed no safe refuge or resting-place in Old England; and having heard that in the Low Countries, as they were then called, there was freedom, or at least toleration, for differences of religious faiths and forms, its members resolved to fly from persecution and establish themselves in Holland. I will not attempt to describe the perils they encountered, and the sufferings they endured, in that flight; — the separations of children from parents, and of wives from husbands; the arrests and examinations, the fines and imprisonments, to which so many of them were subjected; the "hair-breadth 'scapes" of one large party of them during a tempestuous voyage of fourteen days, in crossing the German Ocean, in an almost sinking ship. The whole story is familiar to you. It is enough that we find them all at last safely in Amsterdam, where they are free to enjoy their pure and simple worship, and where they remain quietly for another year.

Not a trace is left of their residence in that then mighty mart, almost a second Venice; born of the sea, "built in the very lap of the floods, and encircled in their watery arms;" and claiming the whole ocean, from the Baltic to the Levant, not only as the field of its enterprise, but almost as its own rightful inheritance and domain. Not a trace of them is left there. We only know that, finding they were in danger of being involved in contentions about women's dresses and men's starched bands, and other such vital matters, which had sprung up in another little church of English Separatists which had fled there before them, and thus of being robbed of that harmony and peace which they prized above all earthly things, and which they had abandoned home and kindred and country to enjoy, — they thought it best to remove once more, and establish themselves at the neighboring inland city of Leyden.

It was a great epoch in Dutch history, when the Pilgrims took up their abode in Holland, and began to habituate themselves to its "strange and uncouth" customs and language. It was the precise period at which, as the close and consummation of "the most tremendous war for liberty ever waged," our own Motley has terminated his admirable account of "The United Netherlands," — to begin it again, we trust, at no distant day, and then to show us precisely what was going on in that interesting country while our Fathers were witnesses and partakers of its fortunes. Within a year after they reached Amsterdam, and the very year they removed to Leyden, the grand twelve years' truce between Spain and her revolted Colonies had been negotiated and ratified. Those Colonies had now virtually established their freedom and independence. Olden Barneveldt and Prince Maurice had reconciled their animosities and rivalries for a time;

and the great Republic — henceforth, though not for ever, to be known and recognized as the United States of the Netherlands — was enjoying internal as well as external peace and rest, after a fearful struggle of forty years' duration.

It is a charming coincidence, certainly, that the coming of the Pilgrims was thus simultaneous with the commencement of that blessed truce, which was destined, too, by its own limitation, to last during the precise period of their stay there. One might almost picture the bow of peace and promise, lifting itself in all its many-colored glories, and overarching that blood-stained soil, to welcome the little band of fugitives for conscience' sake to their temporary repose, and to assure them that war should crimson its fields no more while they should bless it with their presence!

At Leyden, they find, as Bradford says, "a fair and beautiful city, and of a sweet situation, but made more famous by the University wherewith it is adorned, in which of late had been so many learned men." That was, certainly, a noble University, erected as a monument to the heroism of those who had fought and fallen in the dreadful siege which the city had endured so grandly in 1574, — erected in the same spirit in which our Memorial Hall has recently been founded at Cambridge by the Alumni of Harvard. Famous professors, and famous scholars also, it had indeed enjoyed. The learned

Arminius had died just as the Pilgrims arrived there, but his teachings and doctrines were left to be the subject of endless disputation. The marvellous Joseph Scaliger, too, had died the same year; but his not less marvellous pupil, Hugo Grotius, was only at the outset of his great career, having published his Latin Tragedy, "The Suffering Christ," the very year of their arrival at Amsterdam, and his "Mare Liberum" the year of their removal to Leyden.

The youthful Bradford may not, perhaps, have been much in the way of taking note or notice of what was going on at this great seat of learning, as, in default of other means of support, he had put himself as an apprentice to a French Protestant, and was acquiring the art of dyeing silk. But Brewster had found employment as a tutor to some of the youth of the city and the University, and was teaching them the English language by a grammar of his own construction; while, at the same time, he had set up a printing-press, and " was instrumental in publishing several books against the hierarchy, which could not obtain a license in England." To him the University and its learned professors, and all their proceedings and lectures, must have been as familiar as they were interesting. His revered friend and pastor, Robinson, moreover, — as we learn from the researches of an accomplished and lamented New England scholar and traveller (the late Mr.

George Sumner), — was formally admitted to the privileges of a member or subject of the University four or five years after his arrival at Leyden. By the investigations of Mr. Sumner, too, and of a late American Minister at the Hague, the Hon. Henry C. Murphy, we have been enabled to identify the very spot, in the Cathedral Church of St. Peter, where the precious remains of this holy man, whose memory is so dear to New England, were at least temporarily deposited; while the record of that burial has also most happily helped us to fix the exact place of his residence as long as he lived there. In that residence, — and not in any church edifice, for they had none, — there is the best reason for thinking that the Pilgrims worshipped; and thanks to the pious pains of the Rev. Henry Martyn Dexter, of Boston, whose labors in the cause of Pilgrim history I may find further cause for acknowledging, a plate has been affixed to the walls of the building which now stands on that site, inscribed, "On this spot lived, taught and died, JOHN ROBINSON, 1611–1625."

I cannot forget that I lingered in Leyden, for some hours, two or three years ago, for the single purpose of visiting that site, and the place of the grave of him who made it so memorable for ever; but I could find no one at hand to point either of them out for me; and, but for the record of Mr. Sumner and the inscription of Dr. Dexter, I might have missed all that there is there to recall the memory of the Fathers of New England. For, indeed, this is all, — the place of a temporary grave and the site of a dwelling long ago levelled to the ground, — this is absolutely all which can be identified of the Pilgrims' home at Leyden for eleven years. Yet no New Englander, I think, can visit that city on an early autumn or a late summer's day, and behold the ancient buildings on which their eyes must have been accustomed to look; and gaze on the countless canals, and on the flowing river, on the bosom of which they must so often have sailed, and on the banks of which they must so often have rested ; and drink in that soft, hazy, golden sunshine, which one of the great masters of that region (Cuyp), not far from the very time and place at which they were enjoying it, was engaged in making the chief charm of not a few of his most exquisite landscapes, — without being conscious of the inspiration of the scene; nor without feeling and acknowledging that there is, and will for ever be, a magnetic sympathy between Leyden and Plymouth Rock, which no material batteries or tangible wires are needed to kindle and keep alive.

Leyden must indeed have been, as we know it was, most dear to the hearts of the Pilgrim Fathers. There they found rest and safety. There, to use their own language, they enjoyed " much sweet and delightful society and spiritual comfort together in the ways of God," and "lived together in peace and love and holiness." But there, too, they were joined by not a few of those who were to be most serviceable and most dear to them in their future experiences and trials.

There they were joined by JOHN CARVER, of whom we know enough for his own glory, and for his perpetual remembrance among men, in knowing almost nothing except that he was counted worthy to be chosen the first Governor of the little band, and that he died, here at Plymouth, after a brief career, in the faithful discharge of that office.

There ROBERT CUSHMAN joined them, who, in spite of some infirmities of temper and some infelicities of conduct, and though at one time he seemed to have "put his hand to the plough and to have looked back," and was missing from the group whose advent we celebrate to-day, came over not long afterwards, reinstated in the confidence of those with whom he had been so prominently associated at Leyden; delivered, in the Common House of the Plantation, that memorable sermon on Self-Love, the first printed sermon of New England, if not of our whole continent; and, after a perhaps premature return home, continued to watch carefully over the interests of the Pilgrims in England, writing letters remarkable alike for the beauty of their style and for the prudence of their counsel; and was lamented by Bradford, when he heard of his death in 1624, as "a wise and faithful friend."

There they were joined by MILES STANDISH, the intrepid soldier and famous captain of New England; who, having served on the side of the Dutch in the armies of England in the war against Spain, and having now been released by the great truce from further campaigning in the Old World, united himself with the Pilgrims, and, though not a member of their church, followed their fortunes, and fought their battles gallantly to the end. A little man himself, — hardly more than five feet high, — the grand army with which he performed "his most capital exploit" was probably the smallest which was ever mustered for a serious conflict in the annals of human warfare, — only eight men besides their leader. But, "in small room large heart inclosed," he had acquired, not perhaps from Cæsar's Commentaries, his favorite study, but certainly from some other source, a knowledge which some of the ruthless warriors of the present day have failed to exhibit, — the knowledge where to stop, as well as when to strike; and, having secured a signal victory, he brought home in safety every man whom he carried out. Honor to Miles Standish, "the stalwart captain of Plymouth," of whose restrained wrath, when the Puritan influence had come in to temper the profanity for which there was a proverbial license in Flanders, our charming

Longfellow would seem to have caught the very accent and cadence, when he says of it, —

> "Sometimes it seemed like a prayer, and sometimes it sounded like swearing;"

and whose threefold accomplishments he so tersely sums up, when he describes him as doubting

> "Which of the three he should choose for his consolation and comfort,
> Whether the wars of the Hebrews, the famous campaigns of the Romans,
> Or the artillery practice, designed for belligerent Christians."

A higher tribute to the fidelity, vigilance, and courage of the old Plymouth captain could hardly have been paid, than when the late venerable Judge Davis, — a Plymouth man, and full of the original Plymouth spirit, — not many years before his death, unwilling to be wanting to the volunteer patrol service, in Boston, on some occasion of real or imaginary peril, made solemn application to our old Massachusetts Historical Society for the use of one of his reputed — albeit somewhat rusty — swords, and walked the midnight round with that for his trusty and all-sufficient companion.

But there, too, at Leyden, they were joined, — by the accidents of travel, as it would seem, — in 1617, by one of the very noblest of our little band, who was soon associated most leadingly and lovingly with all their spiritual as well as temporal concerns; their Governor for three years, when Bradford had "by importunity got off;" the narrator and chronicler of not a few of the most interesting passages of their history; the leader of not a few of their most important enterprises; a man of eminent activity, resolution, and bravery; who did not shrink from offering himself as a hostage to the savages, while a conference was held and a treaty made with one of their barbarous chieftains; who did not shrink from imprisonment, and the danger of death, in confronting, as an agent of Plymouth and Massachusetts, the tyrannical Archbishop Laud; who earned a gentler and more practical title to remembrance as the importer of the first neat cattle ever introduced into New England; an earnest and devoted friend to the civilization of the Indian tribes and their conversion to Christianity; the chief commissioner of Oliver Cromwell in his warlike designs upon an island, which our own hero President has so recently attempted to secure by peaceful purchase:—EDWARD WINSLOW,— the only one of the Pilgrim Fathers of whom we have an authentic portrait; whose old seat of Careswell, at Marshfield, was the chosen home of Webster; and whose remains, had they not been committed to the deep, when he died so sadly on the sea, at the close of his unsuccessful expedition to St. Domingo, would have been counted among the most precious dust which New England could possess.

Leyden must indeed have been dear to the Pilgrims, as the place where so many of these leading spirits first entered into their association, and first pledged their lives and fortunes to the sacred enterprise.

But Leyden, and the whole marvellous land of which it was at that day one of the most interesting and enlightened cities, had a charm for our Forefathers far above all mere personal considerations. It was a land to which the great German poet, dramatist, and historian, Schiller, in his " Revolt of the Netherlands," gave the noblest testimony, in saying that " every injury inflicted by a tyrant gave a right of citizenship in Holland." It was a land to which that quaint old Suffolk County essayist, Owen Felltham, paid a still higher tribute when he described it as "a place of refuge for sectaries of all denominations." " Let but some of our Separatists be asked," said he, with evident reference to our English exiles of whom he was a contemporary, " let but some of our Separatists be asked, and they shall swear that the Elysian Fields are there." " If you are unsettled," says he in another place, " if you are unsettled in your religion, you may try here all, and take at last what you like best. If you fancy none, you have a pattern to follow of two that would be a church by themselves."

Yes, that was exactly it, — "a Church by themselves;" and there, in that church by themselves, our Pilgrim Fathers first tasted the sweets of civil and religious freedom, and enjoyed that liberty to worship God, according to the dictates of their own consciences, which to them was worth every sacrifice and above all price. There, too, just as they removed from Amsterdam to Leyden, the extraordinary sound was heard, — from the lips of a Roman Catholic, and in behalf of his Roman Catholic brethren, — of an appeal for liberty of conscience which was never surpassed by the founders of Rhode Island, Maryland, or Pennsylvania. "Those," said President Jeannin, most forcibly and eloquently, on taking leave of the States General, "those cannot be said to share any enjoyment from whom has been taken the power of serving God according to the religion in which they were brought up. On the contrary, no slavery is more intolerable nor more exasperates the mind than such restraint. You know this well, my Lords States; you know, too, that it was the principal, the most puissant cause that made you fly to arms and scorn all dangers, in order to effect your deliverance from this servitude. You know that it has excited similar movements in various parts of Christendom, and even in the kingdom of France, with such fortunate success everywhere as to make it appear that God had so willed it, in order to prove that religion ought to be taught and inspired by the movements which come from the Holy Ghost, and not by the force of man."

We know not precisely how far the ears of the

Pilgrims may have been regaled, and their hearts encouraged and strengthened, by this grand appeal from so unaccustomed a source. Brewster, who, as we have seen, had been in the Low Countries before, as Secretary to the English Ambassador, may hardly have been ignorant of it. But, at all events, it affords most significant testimony to the spirit of religious liberty which pervaded the land in which such words at that period could have been uttered; and, coming from the lips of a Romanist, it must have put to shame any Protestant bigotry or intolerance, if any such were lurking there, which might have restrained the full freedom of our English exiles. Dr. Belknap, in his American Biography, may, perhaps, have anticipated events in stating, as he does, that Robinson himself, about this time, after a friendly conference with one upon whose name he had recently made a petulant pun, in an angry controversy, — changing it reproachfully from Ames to *Amiss*, — relaxed the rigor of his Separatism; published a book, allowing and defending the lawfulness of communicating with the Church of England; "allowed pious members of the Church of England, and of all the reformed churches, to communicate with his church; and declared that he separated from no church, but from the corruptions of all churches." But the statement was substantially true of a later period, if not of this. The book, he adds, gained him the title of a Semi-Separatist, and was so offensive to the rigid Brownists of Amsterdam that they would scarcely hold communion with the Church of Leyden.

But, alas! more serious dissensions than these were soon to agitate again that whole united Republic, and to involve it in a crime of which all the multitudinous seas which surround it could hardly wash out the stain. The successor to the chair of Arminius in the University of Leyden (Vorstius) had not only stirred up " hearts of controversy " in his own land by teaching and preaching the peculiar doctrines of his master, but had roused the special indignation of the Royal theological polemic and titular Defender of the Faith across the channel, — that same James I., who a few years before had cut short a conference with the Puritan leaders, at Hampton Court, by declaring that " he would make them conform or he would harry them out of the land," and who, in this respect certainly, had been as good as his word. The recent assassination of his glorious fellow-sovereign, Henry IV. of France, had revived and quickened his antipathy not to Roman Catholics only, but to all religionists who did not agree with himself; and he had the insolence now to demand that the obnoxious Professor of Leyden should be dismissed from his chair and banished from the States, — leaving it, also, to their " Christian wisdom " whether he should not be burned at the stake for " his atheism and blasphemies." The States were compelled to comply, and did most humiliatingly comply, with this demand; but the banishment of Vorstius only the more inflamed the theological strife which raged throughout their dominions. Prince Maurice and Olden Barneveldt were again at each other's throats; the former as the leader of the Calvinist party, and the latter as the leader of the Arminians, with Grotius as his second. And, incredible as it seems to us at this hour, the controversy was only terminated by one of the most infamous judicial murders which pollute the annals of mankind; taking its loathsome place in the calendar of crime by the side of the execution of Sir Walter Raleigh, the year before, and of Algernon Sydney and Lord William Russell half a century later. On the 13th of May, 1619, Olden Barneveldt, the noble patriot and benefactor, second to no one among the founders of the Republic and the authors of its liberties, was condemned to death and beheaded at the Hague; while Grotius was sentenced to perpetual imprisonment, — from which, however, the ingenuity of his wife happily released him at the end of two years.

I would gladly have found some allusion to these monstrous outrages in some of the journals or letters of the Pilgrims. Occurring, as they did, during the very last year of their residence there, I would gladly believe that some abhorrence of such crimes may have mingled with their motives for seeking another place of refuge. Although their religious sympathies were strongly with the Calvinist party, and their pastor, Robinson, had disputed publicly against the doctrines of Arminius, — putting his antagonist Episcopius, the Arminian Professor, to "an apparent nonplus," as Bradford tells us, "not once only, but a second and third time, before a great and public audience, and winning a famous victory for the truth," and "much honor and respect for those who loved the truth," — yet he and Brewster and Bradford and Winslow must have shrunk with horror from this atrocious murder. There is good reason for believing that Brewster, indeed, left Leyden with his family not many weeks afterwards; and I will not doubt that such events increased the eagerness of them all once more to change the place of their habitation, and hastened their negotiations with the merchant adventurers in London.

But their purpose of quitting Holland had been conceived nearly two years before this terrible tragedy was enacted. As early as the autumn of 1617, Robert Cushman and John Carver had been sent as their agents to attempt an arrangement for their removal to America with the Virginia Company in London; and in 1618 the Church of Leyden — with a view to removing the objections, and conciliating the favor of the King and others — had adopted those memorable Seven Articles, first published in 1856 by our accomplished historian Bancroft, in which the authority of his Majesty and of his Bishops is acknowledged, with an unqualified assent "to the confession of faith published in the name of the Church of England and to every article thereof." The adoption of these " Seven Articles," and the appeals addressed to Sir Edwin Sandys and others by Brewster and Robinson, at length elicited an assurance that "both the King and the Bishops had consented to wink at their departure."

" Conniving at them and winking at their departure" were all the assurances they could wring from Royalty. "To allow or tolerate them by his public authority, under his seal, they found it would not be." And though the Virginia Company were strongly desirous to have them go to America under their auspices, and willing to grant them a patent with as ample privileges as they could grant to any one, the feuds and factions in the council of the Company occasioned such delays that no patent was sealed until the 9th of June, 1619; and, after all the labor and cost of procuring it, it was never made use of. An agreement, however, was entered into with Thomas Weston and other merchant adventurers; the Mayflower was hired to await them at Southampton; the Speedwell was bought to take them over to England, and keep them company afterwards; a day of solemn humiliation was spent, — after a parting sermon from Robinson, who was to remain behind with half the members of his church, — " in pouring out prayers to the Lord with great fervency mixed with abundance of tears," and so they proceeded to Delft Haven; and after another most touching parting scene, all kneeling in prayer and taking leave of each other, "with mutual embraces and many tears," the sail was hoisted, and with a prosperous wind they came in a short time to Southampton. There they found "the bigger ship come from London, lying ready, with all the rest of their company." A few days more are occupied in dealing with their agents and the merchant adventurers; a noble farewell letter from Robinson is received and read; and once more they set sail. A leak in the Speedwell compels them to put in at Dartmouth, and then again, after they had gone above a hundred leagues beyond Land's End, to put back to Plymouth, and to abandon the Speedwell altogether. At last, "these troubles being blown over, and now all being compact together in one ship, they put to sea again with a prosperous wind;" and on the 16th day of September, 1620, Old England is parted from for ever. The Mayflower, and its one hundred and two passengers, have entered on the voyage, which is to end not merely in founding a more memorable Plymouth than that which they left behind, but in laying the corner-stone of a mightier and freer nation than the sun in its circuit had ever before shone upon.

England at the moment took no note of their

departing. Her philosophers and statesmen and poets had not quite yet begun to appreciate the losses which religious persecution was entailing upon her. Lord Bacon, indeed, "the great Secretary of Nature and all learning," as Isaac Walton called him, had already foreshadowed the glory which was to be gained by some of his Suffolk and Lincolnshire neighbors, when, in one of his celebrated essays, he assigned the first place, "in the true marshalling of the degrees of sovereign honor," to the "*conditores imperiorum*,—the founders of States and Commonwealths." But it was more than ten years afterwards before the saintly Herbert published those noted lines, which the Vice-Chancellor of Cambridge had so much hesitation about licensing:—

> " Religion stands on tiptoe in our land,
> Readie to passe to the American strand."

And it was nearly ten years later still, when John Milton, in his treatise " Of Reformation in England," exclaimed, " What numbers of faithful and free-born Englishmen, and good Christians, have been constrained to forsake their dearest home, their friends and kindred, whom nothing but the wide ocean, and the savage deserts of America, could hide and shelter from the fury of the bishops! Oh, sir, if we could but see the shape of our dear mother England, as poets are wont to give a personal form to what they please, how would she appear, think ye, but in a mourning weed, with ashes upon her head, and tears abundantly flowing from her eyes, to behold so many of her children exposed at once, and thrust from things of dearest necessity, because their conscience could not assent to things which the bishops thought indifferent!"

But the time was to come when England was to make signal recognition of this memorable Exodus. Little did they imagine, — those pious, humble, simple-hearted men and women, as they stood on the deck of their little bark of only one hundred and eighty tons' burthen, and looked wistfully upon their native shores receding from their moistened eyes, — little did they imagine that the scene of that embarkation, before two centuries and a half had passed away, should not only be among the most cherished ornaments of the Rotundo of the American Capitol, but should be found, as it is found this day, among the most conspicuous frescoes in the corridors of the Parliament Houses of Old England. Still less could the haughty Monarch and the bigoted Prelates, who had reluctantly been induced "to connive and wink at their departure," have dreamed, that such a picture should ever be warranted and welcomed by their successors, as one of the appropriate scenes for inspiring and for warning them, as they should sweep along, through the grand galleries of State, to their places on the throne or the Episcopal bench, in that gorgeous Chamber of the temporal and spiritual Lords of Great Britain.

But this would not be the only souvenir of the Pilgrim Fathers which might suffuse the cheeks of a Bancroft, a Wren, or a Laud, could they be permitted to revisit the scenes of their old prelatical intolerance and arrogance.

The suburban residence of the Bishop of London at Fulham has many charms. Its velvet lawn, its walks upon the Thames, its grand old oaks and cedars of Lebanon, its fine historical portraits, its rare library, its beautiful modern chapel, and, above all, its antique hall, recently restored, — in which the cruel Bonner and the noble Ridley may have successively held their councils during the struggles of the Reformation, and where Bancroft and Laud may have concerted their schemes of bigotry and persecution,— render it altogether one of the most interesting places near London, and hardly less attractive than Lambeth itself. I have been privileged to visit it on more than one of those delicious afternoons of an English June, when the apartments and the grounds were thronged by all that was most distinguished in the society of the Metropolis, assembled to pay their respects to one whose exalted character, and earnest piety, and liberal churchmanship, and unsparing devotion to the humblest as well as the highest duties of his station, have won for him universal esteem, respect, and affection, and who has recently been called by the Queen to the Primacy of all England. But I need hardly say, that to an American, or certainly to a New England eye, there was nothing in all the treasures of art, or of antiquity, or of literature, which that palace contained, — nothing in all the loveliness of its natural scenery and surroundings, nothing in all the historical associations of the spot, nothing in all the beauty and accomplishments and titled or untitled celebrity of the company gathered beneath the roof or scattered upon the lawn, — which could compare for a moment with the interest of an old manuscript volume, which strangely enough had found its way there, of all places in the world, and which had rested for three quarters of a century almost unidentified and unrecognized on its library-shelves. You will all have anticipated me when I say that it is the long-lost manuscript volume, of which but a small portion had ever been printed or copied, written by the hand of William Bradford himself, and giving the detailed story of the Pilgrim Fathers from their first gathering at Scrooby down to the year 1647.

My valued friend, Mr. Charles Deane, to whom, above almost all others, we are indebted for throwing light upon the early history of New England, in the edition of this volume which he so admirably prepared and annotated for the Collections of the Massachusetts Historical Society, has sufficiently described the circumstances of its discovery. When the glad tidings first reached us, I did not fail to sympathize with those who felt that a more rightful as well as more congenial and appropriate place for such a manuscript might be found on this side of the Atlantic. But after a little more reflection, and after we had secured an exact and complete transcript of it for publication, I could not help feeling that there was something of special fitness and felicity in its being left precisely where it is. There let it rest, as a remembrancer to all who shall succeed, generation after generation, to that famous See and its charming palace, of the simple faith, the devoted piety, the brave obedience to the dictates of conscience, of those who led the way in the colonization of New England, and who endured so heroically the persecutions and perils which that great enterprise involved!

How it would have gratified the honest heart of Bradford himself, could he have known where his precious volume should at length be found, and in what estimation it should be held after it was found! How it would have delighted him to know that instead of being set down in some " Index Expurgatorius," or burned at St. Paul's Cross, as compounded of heresy and blasphemy, — as it would have been by those who dwelt or congregated at Fulham at the time it was written, — it should be sacredly guarded among the heirlooms of the palace and its successive occupants! How much more it would have delighted him to know that so much of the simplicity and liberality of form and faith which it portrayed and inculcated, would be cherished and exemplified by more than one of those under whose official custody it was in these latter days to fall!

Few persons, I presume, will doubt that had the Church of England, between 1608 and 1620, been what it is to-day, and its Bishops and Archbishops such in life and in spirit as those who have recently presided at London and Canterbury, Brewster and Bradford would hardly have left Scrooby, and the Mayflower might long have been employed in less interesting ways than in bringing Separatists to Plymouth Rock. As that church and its prelates then were, let us thank God that such Separatists were found! An Episcopalian myself, by election as well as by education, and warmly attached to the forms and the faith in which I was brought up; believing that the Church of England has rendered inestimable service to the cause of religion in furnishing a safe and sure anchorage in so many stormy times, when the minds of men were "tossed to and fro, and carried about with every wind of doctrine;" and prizing that very prayer-book, — which was disowned and discarded by Bradford and Brewster, and by Winthrop, too, — as second only to the Bible in the richness of its treasures of prayer and praise; I yet rejoice, as heartily as any Congregationalist who listens to me, that our Pilgrim Fathers were Separatists.

I rejoice, too, that the Puritan Fathers of Massachusetts, who followed them to these shores ten years afterwards, — though, to the last, they " esteemed it their honor to call the Church of England their dear mother, and could not part from their native country, where she specially resideth, without much sadness of heart and many tears," — were, if not technically and professedly, yet to all intents and purposes, Separatists, also; — Semi-Separatists at least, as Robinson himself was called when he wrote and published that book which so offended the Brownists. I rejoice that the prelatical assumptions and tyrannies of that day were resisted. The Church of England would never have been the noble church it has since become, had there been no seasonable protest against its corruptions, its extravagant formalism, and its overbearing intolerance. The earliest Separatists were those who separated from Rome; and when something more than a disposition was manifested to return towards Rome, in almost every thing except the acknowledgment of its temporal supremacy, another separation could not have been, ought not to have been, avoided. A serious renewal of such manifestations at this day, I need not say, would rend the Anglican Church asunder ; and its American daughter would, under similar circumstances, deservedly share its fate. Pretensions of human infallibility need not be proclaimed by an Ecumenical Council in order to be offensive and abhorrent. It does not require a conclave of Cardinals to render assumptions and proscriptions and excommunications odious. Convocations and Conventions, and even Synods and Councils and Conferences, will answer just as well. When so much of the discipline of the English Church was devoted to matters of form and ceremony; when spiritualism was in danger of forgetting its first syllable, and of degenerating into an empty ritualism; when godly ministers were silenced for "scrupling the vestments," or for preaching an evening lecture, and men and women and children were punished for not bowing in the Creed, or kneeling at the altar, or for having family prayers under their own roof, — separation — call it Schism, if you will — was the true resort and the only remedy. For the sake of the church itself, but a thousand-fold more for the sake of Christianity, which is above all churches, it was needful that a great example of such a separation should be exhibited at all hazards and at any sacrifice. The glorious Luther, to whose memory that majestic monument has so recently been erected at Worms, had furnished such an example in his own day and land, and with relation to the church of which he had once been a devoted disciple. No name may be compared with his name in the grand calendar of Separatists. But our Pilgrim Fathers were humble followers in the same path of Protestantism, and thanks be to God that their hearts were inspired and emboldened to imitate his heroic course.

I would not seem too harsh towards those old prelates of the English Church, by whom Pilgrims or Puritans were persecuted. Sir James Mackintosh, I think, has somewhere said, that if the United Netherlands had erected a statue to the real author of all their liberties, it would have been to the Duke of Alva, whose abominable tyranny goaded the Dutch to desperation, and drove them into rebellion. I am not sure that, on this principle, New England might not well include Bancroft and Laud in her gallery of eminent benefactors. We must never forget, however, that almost all great movements are but the resultants of opposing forces; and that, in impressing upon them their final shape and direction, those who resist are hardly less effective than those who support and urge. Nor can it be forgotten that, in the turn of the wheel of England's fortunes, poor Laud was himself destined to persecution and martyrdom. It must have been a grim joke, when Hugh Peters and others proposed to send him over to New England for punishment, as his Breviate tells us they did; and it might be a matter for curious conjecture what would have happened to him, had he come here then. But the meekness and bravery and Christian heroism with which he bore his fate, when so wantonly and barbarously brought to the block, after four years of imprisonment in the Tower, are almost enough to make us forget that he was ever so haughty and insolent and cruel, and quite enough to extinguish all resentment of his wrongs.

But let me not longer delay to acknowledge, on this occasion, the deep debt which New England and our whole country owes to the Congregationalism which the Pilgrims established on our soil, and of which the very first church in America was planted by them here at Plymouth. My whole heart is in sympathy with the celebration of this Jubilee to be held in my native city, this evening, by the Congregationalists of our land. They would wrong themselves, indeed, as well as all who are not of their own communion, were they to celebrate it in any narrow, controversial spirit, and to turn a national into a merely denominational anniversary. But it would be doing them deep injustice to suggest or imagine such a thing. They have a right to celebrate it, and they will celebrate it, as a day whose associations and influences have far outreached every thing sectarian and every thing sectional, and which are as comprehensive as the land they live in, and as all-embracing as the Christianity they profess and cherish.

Few persons, if any, can hesitate to agree with them, that no other system of church government than Congregationalism could have been successful in New England at that day. No other system could have done so much for religion; no other system could have done so much for liberty, religious or civil. "The meeting-house, the school-house, and the training field," said old John Adams, "are the scenes where New England men were formed." He did not intend to omit the town-house, for no one was more sensible than himself how much of New England education and character was owing to our little municipal organizations, and to the free consultations and discussions of our little town meetings. But he was right in naming "the meeting-house" first. Certainly, for the cause of religious freedom, no other security could have compared with the independent system of church government. Independent churches prepared the way for Independent States and an Independent Nation; and formed the earliest and most enduring barriers and bulwarks at once against hierarchies and monarchies.

That work fully and finally accomplished, and civil and religious freedom securely established, we may all be more than content, we all ought to rejoice, as we witness the association and the prosperous advancement, under whatever name or form they may choose to enroll themselves, of "all who profess and call themselves Christians,"— studying ever, as Edward Winslow tells us the sainted Robinson studied, towards his latter end, "peace and union as far as might agree with faith and a good conscience." Let those who will, indulge in the dream, or cherish the waking vision, of a single universal Church on earth, recognized and accepted of men, whose authority is binding on every conscience and decisive of every point of faith or form. To the eye of God, indeed, such a Church may be visible even now, in "the blessed company of all faithful people," in whatever region they may dwell, with whatever organization they may be connected, with Him as their head, "of whom the whole family in earth and heaven is named." And as, in some grand orchestra, hundreds of performers, each with his own instrument and his own separate score, strike widely variant notes, and produce sounds, sometimes in close succession and sometimes at lengthened intervals, which heard alone would seem to be wanting in every thing like method or melody, but which heard together are found delighting the ear, and ravishing the soul, with a flood of magnificent harmony, as they give concerted expression to the glowing conceptions of some mighty master, like him, the centennial anniversary of whose birthday has just been commemorated,— even so,— even so, it may be,— from the differing, broken, and often seemingly discordant strains of sincere seekers after God, the Divine ear, upon which no lisp of the voice or breathing of the heart is ever lost, catches only a combined and glorious anthem of prayer and praise!

But to human ears such harmonies are not vouchsafed. The Church, in all its majestic unity, shall be revealed hereafter. The "Jerusalem, which is the mother of us all, is above;" and we can only humbly hope that, in the providence of God, its gates shall be wider, and its courts fuller, and its members quickened and multiplied, by the very differences of form and of doctrine which have divided Christians from each other on earth, and which have created something of competition and rivalry, and even of contention, in their efforts to advance the ends of their respective denominations. Absolute religious uniformity, as poor human nature is now constituted, would but too certainly be the cause, if it were not itself the consequence, of absolute religious indifference and stagnation.

Pardon me, fellow-citizens and friends, for a digression, — if it be one, — in which I may almost seem to have forgotten that I have been privileged to occupy this pulpit only for a temporary and secular purpose, and to have encroached on the prerogative of its stated incumbent; but coming here, at your flattering call, to unite in the commemoration of those whose special distinction it was to have separated from the communion to which I rejoice to belong, I could not resist the impulse to give utterance to thoughts which are always uppermost in my mind, when I reflect on this period of New England history. I hasten now to resume and to finish the thread of that Pilgrim narrative which is the legitimate theme of my discourse.

I must not detain you for a moment by the details of that perilous voyage across the Atlantic, with its " many fierce storms, with which the ship was badly shaken and her upper works made very leaky; and one of the mainbeams in the midships bowed and cracked." I must not detain you by dwelling on that " serious consultation " in mid-ocean about putting back, when " the great iron screw which the passengers brought out of Holland " was so providentially found " for the buckling of the main-beam," and " raising it into his place." All this is described in the journal of Bradford with a pathos and a power which could not be surpassed.

I must not detain you either by attempting to portray, in any words of my own, their arrival, on the 21st of November, within the sheltering arm of yonder noble Cape, — " the coast fringed with ice — dreary forests, interspersed with sandy tracts, filling the back ground;"—" no friendly light-houses, as yet, hanging out their cressets on your headlands; no brave pilot boat hovering like a sea-bird on the tops of the waves, to guide the shattered bark to its harbor;. no charts and soundings making the secret pathways of the deep plain as a gravelled road through a lawn." All this was depicted, at the great second-centennial celebration of the settlement of Barnstable, by my lamented friend Edward

Everett, with a grandeur of diction and imagery
which no living orator can approach. They seem
still ringing in my ear from his own lips, — for I
was by his side on that occasion, and no one who
heard him on that day can ever forget his tones or
his words, as, " with a spirit raised above mere
natural agencies," he exclaimed, — " I see the mountains of New England rising from their rocky
thrones. They rush forward into the ocean, settling
down as they advance, and there they range themselves, a mighty bulwark around the heaven-directed
vessel. Yes, the everlasting God himself stretches
out the arm of his mercy and his power in substantial manifestation, and gathers the meek company
of his worshippers as in the hollow of his hand!"

Nor will I detain you for a moment on the simple but solemn covenant which the Pilgrim Fathers
formed and signed in the cabin of the Mayflower on
that same 21st of November, — the earliest " original
compact" of self-government of which we have any
authentic record in the annals of our race. That
has had ample illustration on many other occasions,
and has just been the subject of special commemoration by the New England Historic-Genealogical
Society in Boston.

I turn at once to what concerns this day and this
hour. I turn at once to that third exploring party
which left the Mayflower — not quite blown up by
the rashness of a mischievous boy, and still riding

at anchor in Cape Cod harbor — on the 16th of December; and for whose wanderings in search of a final place of settlement our friend Dr. Dexter has supplied so precise a chronological table. I turn to those "ten of our men," with "two of our seamen," and with six of the ship's company, — eighteen in all, — in an open shallop, who, after spending a large part of two days "in getting clear of a sandy point, which lay within less than a furlong of the ship," — "the weather being very cold and hard," two of their number "very sick" and one of them almost "swooning with the cold," and the gunner for a day and a night seemingly "sick unto death," — found "smoother water and better sailing" on the 17th, but "so cold that the water froze on their clothes and made them many times like coats of iron;" who were startled at midnight by "a great and hideous cry," and after a fearful but triumphant "first encounter," early the next morning, with a band of Indians, who assailed them with savage yells and showers of arrows, and after a hardly less fearful encounter with a furious storm, which "split their mast in three pieces," and swept them so far upon the breakers that the cry was suddenly heard from the helmsman, "About with her, or else we are all cast away," found themselves at last, when the darkness of midnight had almost overtaken them, "under the lee of a small island, and remained all that night in safety," "keeping their watch in the rain."

There they passed the 19th, exploring the island, and perhaps repairing their shattered mast. The record is brief but suggestive: "Here we made our rendezvous all that day, being Saturday." But briefer still, and how much more suggestive and significant, is the entry of the following day! —

"10. (20) of December, on the Sabboth day wee rested."

I pause, — I pause for a moment, — at that most impressive record. Among all the marvellous concisenesses and tersenesses of a Thucydides or a Tacitus, — condensing a whole chapter of philosophy, or the whole character of an individual or a people, into the compass of a motto, — I know of nothing terser or more condensed than this; nor any thing which develops and expands, as we ponder it, into a fuller or finer or more characteristic picture of those whom it describes. "On the Sabbath day we rested." It was no mere secular or physical rest. The day before had sufficed for that. But alone, upon a desert island, in the depths of a stormy winter; well-nigh without food, wholly without shelter; after a week of such experiences, such exposure and hardship and suffering, that the bare recital at this hour almost freezes our blood; without an idea that the morrow should be other or better than the day before; with every conceivable motive, on their own account, and on account of those whom they had left in the ship, to lose not an instant of time, but to hasten and hurry forward to the completion of the work of exploration which they had undertaken, — they still "remembered the Sabbath day to keep it holy." "On the Sabbath day we rested."

It does not require one to sympathize with the extreme Sabbatarian strictness of Pilgrim or Puritan, in order to be touched by the beauty of such a record and of such an example. I know of no monument on the face of the earth, ancient or modern, which would appeal more forcibly to the hearts of all who reverence an implicit and heroic obedience to the commandments of God, than would an unadorned stone on yonder Clark's island, with the simple inscription, "20 Dec. 1620 — On the Sabbath day we rested." There is none to which I would myself more eagerly contribute. But it should be paid for by the penny contributions of the Sabbath-school children of all denominations throughout the land, among whom that beautiful Jubilee Medal has just been distributed.

And what added interest is given to that record, what added force to that example, by the immediate sequel! The record of the very next day runs, — "On Monday we sounded the harbour and found it a very good harbour for our shipping; we marched also into the land, and found divers corn-fields and little running brooks, a place very good for situation; so we returned to our ship again with good news to the rest of our people, which did much comfort their hearts."

That was the day, my friends, which we are here to commemorate. On that Monday, the 21st of December, 1620, from a single shallop, those "ten of our men," with "two of our seamen," and with six of the ship's company, landed upon this shore. The names of almost all of them are given, and should not fail of audible mention on an occasion like this. Miles Standish heads the roll. John Carver comes second. Then follow William Bradford, Edward Winslow, John Tilley, Edward Tilley, John Howland, Richard Warren, Steven Hopkins, and Edward Dotey. The "two of our seamen" were John Alderton and Thomas English; and the two of the ship's company whose names are recorded were Master Copin and Master Clarke, from the latter of whom the Sabbath island was called.

They have landed. They have landed at last, after sixty-six days of weary and perilous navigation since bidding a final farewell to the receding shores of their dear native country. They have landed at last; and when the sun of that day went down, after the briefest circuit of the year, New England had a place and a name — a permanent place, a never to be obliterated name — in the history, as well as in the geography, of civilized Christian man.

> "They whom once the desert beach
> Pent within its bleak domain, —
> Soon their ample sway shall stretch
> O'er the plenty of the plain!"

I will not say that the corner-stone of New England had quite yet been laid. But its symbol and perpetual synonyme had certainly been found. That one grand Rock, — even then without its fellow along the shore, and destined to be without its fellow on any shore throughout the world, — Nature had laid it, — The Architect of the Universe had laid it, — " when the morning stars sang together, and all the sons of God shouted for joy." There it had reposed, unseen of human eye, the storms and floods of centuries beating and breaking upon it. There it had reposed, awaiting the slow-coming feet, which, guided and guarded by no mere human power, were now to make it famous for ever. The Pilgrims trod it, as it would seem, unconsciously, and left nothing but authentic tradition to identify it. "Their rock was not as our rock." Their thoughts at that hour were upon no stone of earthly mould. If they observed at all what was beneath their feet, it may indeed have helped them still more fervently to lift their eyes to Him who had been predicted and promised " as the shadow of a great rock in a weary land;" and may have given renewed emphasis to the psalm which perchance they may have recalled, — " From the end of the earth will I cry unto thee, when my heart is overwhelmed: lead me to the rock that is higher than I." Their trust was only on the Rock of Ages.

We have had many glowing descriptions and not

a few elaborate pictures of this day's doings; and it has sometimes been a matter of contention whether Mary Chilton or John Alden first leapt upon the shore, — a question which the late Judge Davis proposed to settle by humorously suggesting that the friends of John Alden should give place to the lady, as a matter of gallantry. But the Mayflower, with John Alden, and Mary Chilton, and all the rest of her sex, and all the children, was still in the harbor of Cape Cod. The aged Brewster, also, was on board the Mayflower with them; and sorely needed must his presence and consolation have been, as poor Bradford returned to the ship, after a week's absence, to find that his wife had fallen overboard and was drowned the very day after his departure.

I may not dwell on these or any other details, except to recall the fact that on Friday, the 25th, they weighed anchor, — it was Christmas Day, though they did not recognize it, as so many of us are just preparing to recognize it, as the brightest and best of all the days of the year; — that on Saturday, the 26th, the Mayflower "came safely into a safe harbour;" and that on Monday, the 28th, the landing was completed. Not only was the time come and the place found, but the whole company of those who were for ever to be associated with that time and that place were gathered at last where we are now gathered to do homage to their memory.

I make no apology, sons and daughters of New

England, for having kept always in the foreground of the picture I have attempted to draw, the religious aspects and incidents of the event we have come to commemorate. Whatever civil or political accompaniments or consequences that event may have had, it was in its rise and progress, in its inception and completion, eminently and exclusively a religious movement. The Pilgrims left Scrooby as a church. They settled in Amsterdam and in Leyden as a church. They embarked in the Mayflower as a church. They came to New England as a church; and Morton, at the close of the introduction to Bradford's History, as given by Dr. Young in his Chronicles, entitles it " The Church of Christ at Plymouth in New England, first begun in Old England, and carried on in Holland and Plymouth aforesaid." They had no license, indeed, from either Pope or Primate. It was a church not only without a bishop, but without even a pastor; with only a layman to lead their devotions and administer their discipline. A grand layman he was, — Elder Brewster: it would be well for the world if there were more laymen like him, at home and abroad. In yonder Bay, it is true, before setting foot on Cape Cod, they entered into a compact of civil government; but the reason expressly assigned for so doing was, that "some of the strangers amongst them (*i. e.*, not Leyden men, but adventurers who joined them in England) had let fall in the ship that when they came ashore they would use their own liberty, for none had power to command them," or, as elsewhere stated, because they had observed " some not well affected to unity and concord, but gave some appearance of faction." They came as a Church: all else was incidental, the result of circumstances, a protection against outsiders. They came to secure a place to worship God according to the dictates of their own consciences, free from the molestations and persecutions which they had encountered in England; and free, too, from the uncongenial surroundings, the irregular habits of life, the strange and uncouth language, the licentiousness of youth, the manifold temptations, and " the neglect of observation of the Lord's day as a Sabbath," which they had so lamented in Holland.

We cannot be too often reminded that it was religion which effected the first permanent settlement in New England. All other motives had failed. Commerce, the fisheries, the hope of discovering mines, the ambition of founding Colonies, all had been tried, and all had failed. But the Pilgrims asked of God; and "He gave them the heathen for their inheritance, and the uttermost parts of the earth for their possession." Religious faith and fear, religious hope and trust, — the fear of God, the love of Christ, an assured faith in the Holy Scriptures, and an assured hope of a life of bliss and blessedness to come, — these, and these alone, proved sufficient to animate and strengthen them for the endurance of all the toils and trials which such an enterprise involved. Let it never be forgotten that if the corner-stone of New England was indeed laid by the Pilgrim Fathers, two centuries and a half ago to-day, it was in the cause of religion they laid it; and whatever others may have built upon it since, or may build upon it hereafter, — "gold, silver, precious stones, wood, hay, stubble," — God forbid that on this Anniversary the foundation should be ignored or repudiated!

As we look back ever so cursorily on the great procession of American History as it starts from yonder Rock, and winds on and on and on to the present hour, we may descry many other scenes, many other actors, remote and recent, in other parts of the Union as well as in our own, of the highest interest and importance. There are Conant and Endicott with their little rudimental plantations at Cape Ann and at Salem. There is the elder Winthrop, with the Massachusetts Charter, at Boston, of whom the latest and best of New England Historians (Dr. Palfrey) has said "that it was his policy, more than any other man's, that organized into shape, animated with practical vigor, and prepared for permanency, those primeval sentiments and institutions that have directed the course of thought and action in New England in later times." There is the younger Winthrop, not far behind, with the Charter of Connecticut, of whose separate Colonies Hooker and Haynes and Hopkins and Eaton and Davenport and Ludlow had laid the foundations. There is Roger Williams, " the Apostle of soul freedom," as he has been called, with the Charter of Rhode Island. There is the brave and generous Stuyvesant of the New Netherlands. There are the Catholic Calverts, and the noble Quaker Penn, building up Maryland and Pennsylvania alike, upon principles of toleration and philanthropy. There is the benevolent and chivalrous Oglethorpe, assisted by Whitefield and the sainted Wesleys, planting his Moravian Colony in Georgia. There is Franklin, with his first proposal of a Continental Union, and with his countless inventions in political as well as physical science. There is James Otis with his great argument against Writs of Assistance, and Samuel Adams with his inexorable demand for the removal of the British regiments from Boston. There are Quincy with his grand remonstrance against the Port Bill, and Warren, offering himself as the Proto-martyr on Bunker Hill. There is Jefferson with the Declaration of Independence fresh from his own pen, with John Adams close at his side, as its " Colossus on the floor of Congress." There are Hamilton and Madison and Jay bringing forward the Constitution in their united arms; and there, leaning on their shoulders, and on that Constitution, but towering above them all, is WASHINGTON, the consummate commander, the incomparable President, the world-honored Patriot. There are Marshall and Story as the expounders of the Constitution, and Webster as its defender. There is John Quincy Adams with his powerful and persistent plea for the sacred Right of Petition. There is Jackson with his Proclamation against Nullification. There is Lincoln with his ever memorable Proclamation of Emancipation. And there, closing for the moment that procession of the dead, — for I presume not to marshal the living, — is George Peabody, with his world-wide munificence and his countless benefactions. Other figures may present themselves to other eyes as that grand Panorama is unrolled. Other figures will come into view as that great procession advances. But be it prolonged, as we pray God it may be, even " to the crack of doom," first and foremost, as it moves on and on in radiant files, — " scaring the eyeballs " of oppressors and tyrants, but rejoicing the hearts of the lovers of freedom throughout the world, — will ever be seen and recognized the men whom we commemorate to-day, — the Pilgrim Fathers of New England. No herald announces their approach. No pomp or parade attends their advent. "Shielded and helmed and weapon'd with the truth," no visible guards are around them, either for honor or defence. Bravely but humbly, and almost unconsciously, they assume their perilous posts, as pioneers of an advance which is to know no backward steps, until, throughout this Western hemisphere, it shall have prepared the way of the Lord and of liberty. They come with no charter of human inspiration. They come with nothing but the open Bible in their hands, leading a march of civilization and human freedom, which shall go on until time shall be no more, — if only that Bible shall remain open, and shall be accepted and reverenced, by their descendants as it was by themselves, as the Word of God!

It is a striking coincidence that while they were just taking the first steps in the movement which terminated at Plymouth Rock, that great clerical Commission was appointed by King James, which prepared what has everywhere been received as the standard English version of the Holy Scriptures; and which, though they continued to use the Geneva Bible themselves, has secured to their children and posterity a translation which is the choicest treasure of literature as well as of religion. Nor can I fail to remember, with the warmest interest, that, at this moment, while we are engaged in this Fifth Jubilee Commemoration, a similar Commission is employed, for the first time, in subjecting that translation to the most critical revision; — not with a view, certainly, to attempt any change or improvement of its incomparable style and language, but only to purge the sacred volume from every human interpolation or error.

No more beautiful scene has been witnessed in our day and generation, nor one more auspicious of that Christian unity which another world shall witness, if not this, than the scene presented in Westminster Abbey, in the exquisite chapel of Henry VII., by that Revision Commission, in immediate preparation for entering on their great task, on the morning of the 22d of June last;—"such a scene," as the accomplished Dean Alford has well said, "as has not been enacted since the name of Christ was first named in Britain." I can use no other words than his, in describing it: "Between the latticed shrine of King Henry VII. and the flat pavement tomb of Edward VI. was spread 'God's board,' and round that pavement tomb knelt, shoulder to shoulder, bishops and dignitaries of the Church of England, professors of her Universities, divines of the Scottish Presbyterian and Free Churches, and of the Independent, Baptist, Wesleyan, Unitarian Churches in England,—a representative assembly, such as our Church has never before gathered under her wing, of the Catholic Church by her own definition,—of 'all who profess and call themselves Christians.'" It was a scene to give character to an age; and should the commission produce no other valuable fruit, that opening Communion will make it memorable to the end of time.

Yes, the open Bible was the one and all-sufficient

support and reliance of the Pilgrim Fathers. They looked, indeed, for other and greater reformations in religion than any which Luther or Calvin had accomplished or advocated; but they looked for them to come from a better understanding and a more careful study of the Holy Scriptures, and not from any vain-glorious human wisdom or scientific investigations. As their pastor Robinson said, in his farewell discourse, "He was confident the Lord had more truth and light yet to break forth out of his Holy Word."

Let me not seem, my friends, to exaggerate the importance to our country of the event which we this day celebrate. The Pilgrims of the Mayflower did not establish the earliest permanent English settlement within the territories which now constitute our beloved country. I would by no means overlook or disparage the prior settlement at Jamestown in Virginia. The Old Dominion, with all its direct and indirect associations with Sir Walter Raleigh, and with Shakspeare's accomplished patron and friend, the Earl of Southampton, — with Pocahontas, too, and Captain John Smith, — must always be remembered by the old Colony with the respect and affection due to an elder sister. "I said an elder, not a better." Yet we may well envy some of her claims to distinction. More than ten years before an English foot had planted itself on the soil of New England, that Virginia Colony had effected a settlement; and more than a year before the landing of the Pilgrims, — on the 30th of July, 1619, — the first Representative Legislative Assembly ever held within the limits of the United States was convened at Jamestown. That Assembly passed a significant Act against drunkenness; and an Act somewhat quaint in its terms and provisions, but whose influence might not be unwholesome at this day, against "excessive apparel," — providing that every man should be assessed in the church for all public contributions, "if he be unmarried, according to his own apparel; if he be married, according to his own and his wife's, or either of their apparel." Such a statute would have been called puritanical, if it had emanated from a New England Legislature. It might even now, however, do something to diminish the dimensions, and simplify the material, and abate the luxurious extravagance, of modern dress. But that first Jamestown Assembly passed another most noble Act, for the conversion of the Indians and the education of their children, which entitles Virginia to claim pre-eminence, or certainly priority, in that great work of Christian philanthropy, for which our Fathers, with glorious John Eliot at their head, did so much, and for which their sons, alas! have accomplished so little, — unless, perhaps, under the new and noble Indian policy of the last twelve months. The political organization of Virginia was almost mature, while that of New England was still in embryo.

Again, I do not forget that the Pilgrims of the Mayflower built up no great City or Commonwealth. Within the first three months after their landing, one-half of their number had fallen victims to the rigors of the climate and the hardships of their condition; and at the end of ten years the whole population of the Colony — men, women, and children — did not exceed three hundred. They were but as a voice in the desert; but it was a glorious voice, and one which was destined to reverberate around the world, and ring along the ages with still increasing emphasis. Other Colonies, by the inspiration and encouragement of their example, soon succeeded them, and did the substantial work for which they only prepared the way; for which they, as they said themselves, were but "stepping-stones." The great "Suffolk Emigration" of 1630, — "The Governor and Company of the Massachusetts Bay," — coming over in eleven ships, with the whole government and its Charter, were the main founders and builders of the grand old Commonwealth, of which the Plymouth Colony, sixty years afterwards, became an honored part.

It is pleasant to remember how harmoniously and lovingly the two Colonies lived together. It is pleasant to remember that parting charge of John Cotton to the Massachusetts Company, at Southampton, "that they should take advice of them at Plymouth, and do nothing to offend them." I cannot forget, either, the cordial visit of Governor Bradford to Governor Winthrop in 1631; nor that Winthrop soon afterwards subjected himself to reproach for supplying the Pilgrims with powder, at his personal cost, in a moment of their urgent danger and distress. Still less can I forget that October day in 1632, when Governor Winthrop returned Bradford's visit, coming a large part of the way here on foot, and crossing the river on the back of his guide; and when Bradford and Brewster and Roger Williams and Winthrop, with John Wilson, the first pastor of Boston, were together on this spot, engaging in religious discourse, and partaking of the Sacrament together. That most impressive and memorable Communion was at once the harbinger and the pledge, the prediction and the assurance, of the peace and harmony, the co-operation and concord, which were long to prevail between the infant Colonies of New England.

True, there were some shades of difference in the religious sentiment and in the civil administration of the various plantations, as they were successively developed. The charges of intolerance, bigotry, superstition, and persecution, which there seems to have been a special delight, in some quarters, of late years, in arraying against our New England Fathers and founders, apply without doubt more directly to other Colonies, than to that whose landing we this day commemorate. The Pilgrims in their narrow retreat of rock and sand were but little disturbed by " intruders and dissentients," — as my friend Dr. Ellis has so well classified them, — and could afford to be less rigid in their admissions and exclusions. Their leaders, too, were perhaps of a somewhat more lenient and liberal temper than those who settled elsewhere. Let them have all the honor which belongs to them; and let censure and condemnation fall wherever it is deserved! I am not here to justify or excuse all the extravagances, superstitions, or persecutions of the Puritan Colonists. But still less am I here to pander to the prurient malignity of those who are never weary of prying into the petty faults and follies of our Fathers, and who seem to gloat and exult in holding them up to the ridicule and reproach of their children. As if those great hearts, whether of 1620 or 1630, had fled into the wilderness to assert and vindicate a broad, abstract, unqualified doctrine of religious liberty, or even of religious toleration, to which they had afterwards proved recreant themselves! As if the precarious circumstances of their condition — with savage foes watching to extirpate them, with famine ever staring them in the face, with disease and death menacing them in every shape and at every turn — did not constrain and compel them, in the earlier stages of their career, to adopt the principle of excluding from their community any and all who were bent upon introducing contention and discord, and of enforcing among themselves something of that stern martial rule which belongs to a besieged camp! Why, even Roger Williams himself was forced to introduce a right of exclusion, or non-admission, into his original articles of settlement at Providence. We can never too often recall the language of the late venerable Josiah Quincy, — the last man of our day and generation — I had almost said of any day and generation — to palliate real bigotry or wanton intolerance, — when he said, in his masterly Discourse on the Second Centennial Anniversary of the Settlement of Boston in 1630: "Had our early ancestors adopted the course we at this day are apt to deem so easy and obvious, and placed their government on the basis of liberty for all sorts of consciences, it would have been, in that age, a certain introduction of anarchy. . . . The non-toleration which characterized our early ancestors, from whatever source it may have originated, had undoubtedly the effect they intended and wished. It excluded from influence, in their infant settlement, all the friends and adherents of the ancient monarchy and hierarchy; all who, from any motive, ecclesiastical or civil, were disposed to disturb their peace or their churches. They considered it a measure of 'self-defence.' And it is unquestionable that it was chiefly instrumental in forming the homogeneous and exclusively republican character for which the people of New England have, in all times, been distinguished; and, above all, that it fixed irrevocably in the country that noble security for religious liberty, the independent system of Church Government."

But whatever may have been the differences or disagreements of the first planters of Plymouth and Massachusetts Bay, of New Haven and of Connecticut, at the outset, we all know that in the summer of 1643 these four original Colonies established that noble New England Confederation, — the model and prototype of the Confederation of 1778, which "blended the many-nationed whole in one," and carried the thirteen American Colonies through the War of Independence, — whose grand and comprehensive preamble is alone an ample reply to all who would magnify one Colony at the expense of another: —

"Whereas we all came into these parts of America with one and the same end and aim, namely, to advance the Kingdom of our Lord Jesus Christ and to enjoy the liberties of the Gospel in purity with peace: And whereas in our settling (by a wise providence of God) we are further dispersed upon the Seacoasts and Rivers than was at first intended, so that we cannot according to our desire with convenience communicate in one Government and Jurisdiction: And whereas we live encompassed with people of several Nations and strange languages, which hereafter may prove injurious to us or our posterity: And forasmuch as the Natives have formerly committed sundry insolences and outrages upon several plantations of the English, and have of late combined themselves against us: And seeing by reason of those sad distractions in England which they have heard of, and by which they know we are hindered from that humble way of seeking advice, or reaping those comfortable fruits of protection which at other times we might well expect: We therefore do conceive it our bounden duty without delay to enter into a present Consociation amongst ourselves, for mutual help and strength in all our future concernments: That as in Nation and Religion so in other respects we be and continue ONE, according to the tenor and true meaning of the ensuing Articles: Wherefore it is fully agreed and concluded by and between the parties or Jurisdictions above-named, and they jointly and severally do by these presents agree and conclude, That they all be and henceforth be called by the name of The United Colonies of New England."

The very next clause of this remarkable Ordinance provided as follows: "The said United Colonies for themselves and their posterities do jointly and severally hereby enter into a firm and perpetual league of friendship and amity for offence and defence, mutual advice and succour, upon all just occasions both for preserving and propagating the truth and liberties of the Gospel and for their own mutual safety and welfare." And another article provided for intrusting the whole management of the Confederation to two Commissioners from each of the four Jurisdictions, carefully adding, "all in Church fellowship with us," — thus leaving no shadow of doubt upon the point that it was a "Consociation" for religious as well as for political peace and unity.

Accordingly we find among the proceedings of the Commissioners at New Haven in 1646 — a meeting at which neither Bradford nor Winslow nor either of the Winthrops was present, but at which all of the four Colonies were fully represented, and to whose proceedings all of them ultimately subscribed — that most memorable Declaration as to the "Spreading nature of Error and the dangerous growth and effects thereof," "under a deceitful colour of liberty of conscience," which recommended, among other things, that "Anabaptism, Familism, Antinomianism, and generally all errours of a like nature," "be seasonably and duly suppressed;" and which concluded with that glowing prediction for New England: "If thus we be for God, he will certainly be with us; and though the God of the world (as he is styled) be worshipped, and by usurpation set upon his throne in the main and greatest part of America, yet this small part and portion may be vindicated as by the right hand of Jehovah, and justly called Emmanuel's land."

I do not forget that, in reference to the clause recommending the suppression of errors, the Plymouth Commissioners "desired further consideration;" but the whole Declaration is entered upon the Plymouth Records as agreed upon, and was ultimately subscribed alike by the Commissioners of all the Colonies.

I do not forget, either, that all New England was not included in that Confederation. All that there was of New Hampshire was indeed within the jurisdiction of Massachusetts. But we miss Rhode Island from the historic group. We miss Clarke and Coddington and Roger Williams from the roll of the Commissioners. It must be borne in mind, however, that it was not because the Plantations at Providence and the Islands were opposed to the Confederation or any of its articles, that they were not members of it. Both of them desired and solicited admission. "There was yet another, a fifth New England Colony (said John Quincy Adams in 1843), denied admission into the Union, and furnishing, in its broadest latitude, the demonstration of that conscientious, contentious spirit, which so signally characterized the English Puritans of the seventeenth century, the founders of New England, of all the liberties of the British Nation, and of the ultimate universal freedom of the race of man. The founder of the Colony of Rhode Island (adds he) was Roger Williams, a man who may be considered the very impersonation of this combined conscientious, contentious spirit."

Rhode Island may well afford to bear with equanimity any charges against the early contentiousness of her founders, in view of the glory which that very contentiousness has acquired for her on the page of history. " Roger Williams (says Bancroft) was the first person in modern Christendom to assert in its plenitude the doctrine of the liberty of conscience, the equality of opinions before the law; and in its defence he was the harbinger of Milton, the precursor and superior of Jeremy Taylor." The man upon whose tombstone such an inscription, — even with some allowances for rhetorical exaggeration, — may be justly written, need fear no strictures to which other peculiarities of character or conduct may subject him. I have an hereditary disposition, too, to be not only just but tender towards his memory, for Williams and the Winthrops of old, in spite of all differences, were most loving friends from first to last. I would palliate not a particle of the persecution or cruelty which he suffered; from whatever source it may have proceeded, or by whomever it may have been prompted. There was an heroic grandeur in his endurance and fortitude; there was an unsparing self-devotion in his care for the Indians; there was a simplicity, sincerity, and earnestness in his whole career and character, — which must ever command our warmest sympathy and admiration.

But it would be gross injustice to our other New England Fathers, and especially to our Massachusetts Fathers, not to admit that the conduct of Williams, in some of its earlier manifestations, was too precipitate and turbulent to be compatible with the peace and safety of the infant Colonies, — denying, as Winslow says he did, the lawfulness of a public oath, refusing "to allow the colors of our nation," and holding forth the unlawfulness of the patent from the king; — while the condition and temper of the plantations of Rhode Island — a State which we now so honor and love, and to which we owe more than one of our most valued citizens — were such, at that time, as to cause even the Plymouth rulers and elders to say: "Concerning the Islanders, we have no conversing with them, nor desire to have, further than necessity or humanity may require."

But with the exception of these Rhode Island Plantations, which were still very small and scattered, New England was then one; one, not only as the multiplied States of our American Union are one at this day, for civil, political, and military purposes; but one, also, in a unity to which our Federal Constitution presents no counterpart; — one for the preservation and propagation of Religion; a Union for the defence and diffusion of pure, Protestant Christianity, such as the world had hardly ever witnessed before, and may hardly ever witness again. It was a grand Experiment, conceived and instituted for the glory of God and the welfare of man's estate. But a higher than human power had long ago emphatically declared, "My Kingdom is not of this world;" and the result gave abundant evidence that, on this Continent at least, the Temporal and Spiritual power were not destined to be wielded successfully by the same hands. Church and State were never meant to thrive together on American soil. It remains to be seen how long they are to thrive together anywhere.

I hasten to the conclusion of this discourse. I may not attempt to pursue the thread of Pilgrim history further on this occasion. We all know what New England has been doing since the days of that Confederation. We all know how her sons and her daughters, besides founding and building up noble institutions within her own limits, have sought homes in other parts of the country, near and remote, and how powerfully their influence and enterprise have everywhere been felt. It may safely be said that there is hardly a State, or county, or town, or village, on the Continent, in which New England men and women are not turning their faces towards Plymouth Rock to-day with something of the affectionate yearning of children towards an ancestral, or even a parental, home. We all know what contributions they have made to the cause of Education, of Learning, of Literature, of Science, and of Art. We all know what they have done for Commerce on the ocean, and for Industry on the land, vexing every sea with their keels, and startling every waterfall with their looms. We all know what examples of Patriotism and Statesmanship they have exhibited in every hour of Colonial or National trial. We do not fail to remember that New England led the march to Independence at Lexington and Concord and Bunker Hill, and that the bones of her sons were mingled with almost every soil on which the battles of the Revolution were fought. Still less can we forget with what alacrity and heroic self-sacrifice her bravest and best rushed forth, — so many of them, alas! never to return, — for the defence of the Union, in the great struggle which has so recently terminated.

But we are not here to-day to boast of our own exploits, or to deal with the events of our own day. It becomes us rather to remember our own shortcomings and our own unworthiness, in view of the sublime examples of piety, endurance, and heroic valor which were exhibited by those "holy and humble men of heart" by whom our Colonies were planted. We sometimes assume to sit in judgment upon their doings. We often criticise their faults and failings. There is a special proneness of late years to deride their superstitions and denounce their intolerance. And certainly we may well rejoice that the days of religious bigotry and proscription are over in our land. But is it not even more true at this hour, than when no less liberal a Christian than John Quincy Adams uttered the warning, thirty years ago, that the intensely religious feelings and prejudices of our infancy have not only given way to universal toleration, but " to a liberality of doctrine bordering upon the extreme of a faltering faith"? God forbid that our own religious freedom should ever be described as Gibbon described that of the age of Antoninus, from which he dates the decline and fall of the Roman Empire: "The various modes of worship (says he) which prevailed in the Roman world were all considered by the people as equally true; by the philosophers as equally false; and by the magistrates as equally useful. And thus toleration produced not only mutual indulgence, but even religious concord." Such a spirit of toleration, — such religious liberty as that, — even in an age of Paganism, gradually led to the overthrow of the great Empire of the Old

World. What else but overthrow can it accomplish in a Christian age for the great Republic of the New World?

May it not be wise and well for us all sometimes to reflect — and may I not be pardoned for concluding this discourse by summoning the sons and daughters of New England, here and everywhere, to reflect this day — what judgment would be pronounced upon us by our Pilgrim and our Puritan Fathers, could they be permitted to behold and to comprehend the grand expansion and development which we now witness of the institutions which they planted? Could they descend among us, at this moment, in bodily presence, and with organs capable of embracing at a glance a full perception and understanding of every thing which has been accomplished on this wide-spread continent, since they were withdrawn from these earthly scenes and entered into their rest, — what would they think, what would they say?

It is not difficult to imagine the surprise with which they would contemplate the existing condition of New England, and of the mighty nation of which it forms a part. It is not difficult to imagine the astonishment with which they would regard the great inventions and improvements of modern times. It is not difficult to imagine the eager and incredulous amazement with which Miles Standish, for instance, would listen to the click of a little machine, almost at his own old doorway, which could supply him daily and hourly with the latest phases of the big wars in Europe, which in his lifetime he could only have studied in bulletins, or broadsides, or "books of the news," not much less than half a year old. It is not difficult to conceive the wonder of Edward Winslow, as he should see, or be told of, some noble ship traversing the wide Atlantic, from Land's End to Cape Cod, with undeviating regularity, without sails and against the wind, in far less time than he could have relied on crossing from one little island to another of the Caribbean Sea, before he sunk so sadly beneath its waters. It is not difficult to picture the bewilderment of Brewster and Bradford as they should listen to the rattling and whistling and thundering, by day and by night, of cars bringing more passengers than the whole population of Plymouth in their day, and more freight than would have sustained that whole population for a winter, not merely from Boston in not much more than an hour, but from the shores of the Pacific Ocean in not much more than a week! It is easy to conceive the consternation of them all, could they see this whole assembly, by an almost instantaneous flash of sunlight, grouped and pictured with an exactness which the most protracted labors of ancient or modern art could never have reached. It is easy to conceive their rapture should they witness the intensest physical agonies of the human frame charmed to sleep by the inhalation of the vapor of a few drops of ether. It is easy to understand how astounded they would be, not merely at learning that all those phenomena of the celestial bodies which had so often perplexed and alarmed them were now familiar to every school-boy; but at being specially informed that to-morrow there should be a great eclipse of the sun, total in some parts of the world though hardly visible here; and that Science, not satisfied with calculating, by the old processes of which they may have heard something before, the precise instants of its beginning and end, had equipped and sent out formal expeditions to many distant lands to observe and record all its phases and incidents!

We can readily suppose that such marvels as these would not be taken in by them without reawakening something of their old superstitious fear and awe; and we might expect to hear from their lips some exclamations, if not about "the old Serpent," certainly about "wonders and more wonders of the invisible world." But we need not resort to these miracles of science and art in order to illustrate the surprise and amazement with which our Fathers would contemplate the condition of their posterity. The mere extent, population, and power of our country, its great States, its magnificent cities, its vast wealth, its commerce, its crops, its industry, its education, its freedom, — no longer a slave upon its soil, — all, all of all races, equal before the law, — what else could they desire to fill up the measure of our development, or of their own delight! What more could they possibly wish to complete and crown the vision of glory vouchsafed to them?

Oh, my friends, have you forgotten, or can you imagine that they would forget for an instant, the cause in which they came here? Can you believe that they would be so dazzled and blinded by the glare of mere temporal success and material prosperity, or by the grandeur of intellectual triumphs and scientific discoveries and philosophical achievements, as to lose sight and thought of that which animated — and, I had almost said, constituted — their whole mortal existence? Can we not hear them inquiring eagerly and earnestly, as they gaze upon all around them, " Is the moral welfare of the country keeping pace with its material progress? Has religion maintained the place we assigned it, as the corner-stone of all your institutions? Is the Bible, the open Bible, which we brought over in our hands, still reverenced of you all as the Word of God? Is the Lord's Day still respected and observed as a day of religious rest, as we observed it on that desolate island before our feet had stept upon yonder consecrated rock? Are your houses of worship proportionate to your population? Are there worshippers enough, Sunday by Sunday, to fill the houses which you have? Are there no temples of false prophets — no organized communities of licentiousness, under the color of religion — in your land? Are there none among you who 'seek unto them that have familiar spirits and unto wizards that peep and that mutter, — for the living to the dead'? Are you doing your full part in carrying the Gospel to the heathen? Or are you waiting until the heathen shall have come over into your inheritance, bringing their idols with them, to cheapen labor and to dilute your own civilization and Christianity? Are your schools and colleges still dedicated, as we dedicated at least one of them, 'to Christ and the Church'? Is there no fear that your science has been emboldened by its triumphant successes to overleap the bounds of legitimate investigation, putting Nature to the rack to wring from her, if it were possible, some denial, or some doubt, of that great Original, whom she has always rejoiced, and still rejoices, to proclaim? Is there no fear that your philosophy has been tempted to transcend the just 'limits of religious thought,' and to set up some material theory, or some self-styled positive system, which may seduce the deluded soul from its hope of immortality, and weaken, if not destroy, its sense of the need of a Saviour? Is there no fear that a sentimental, sensational, licentious literature is corrupting the tastes and sapping the morals of your children, and rendering the universal appetite for reading an almost doubtful blessing? Are your charities, public and private, numerous and noble as they are, altogether commensurate with your wealth? Or is the larger half of your surplus incomes absorbed in a cankering and debasing luxury, destructive alike to the physical, intellectual, and spiritual energy of all who indulge in it? Are integrity and virtue enthroned in your hearts and homes? Have they a recognized and undisputed sovereignty in the market-place and on the exchange? Or are vice and crime making not a few days dark, and not a few nights hideous, in your crowded cities? Is there purity and principle and honor in your public servants? Or are corruption and intrigue and fraud threatening to make havoc of your free institutions, rendering all things venal, and almost all things, except mere party disloyalty, venial, in your State and National Capitals?"

Such questions as these, I am conscious, if coming from any living lips, or, certainly, from any living layman's lips, might be jeered at as savoring of sanctimoniousness and fanaticism. I do not presume to ask them for myself; much less would I presume to answer them. Make what allowance you please for the rigid austerity and excessive scrupulousness of those for whom I am only an interpreter. But does any one deny or doubt that they are the very questions which would be asked first, and most eagerly and most emphatically, by those whom we this day commemorate, and by those who were associated with them in founding and building up New England?

Can we not hear them, at this moment, solemnly warning us, lest, in the pride of our prosperity and greatness, "when our silver and our gold is multiplied, and all that we have is multiplied," our hearts be lifted up to say, each for himself, "My power and the might of mine hand hath gotten me this wealth," while the great lesson of our stewardship, to Him to whom we owe it all, is forgotten or neglected?

Can we not hear them, at this moment, solemnly warning us, lest, in the pride of our freedom and independence, we forget that "the liberty we are to stand for, with the hazard not only of our goods, but of our lives if need be," is "a liberty for that only which is good, just, and honest," and not a liberty to be used as a cloak of maliciousness and licentiousness?

Can we not hear them, at this moment, from yonder hill of graves, solemnly and affectionately warning us lest, in the pride of our science, while a thousand telescopes and spectroscopes are ready to be levelled, on the morrow, at the orb of day, — to reveal its chromosphere and its photosphere, to measure its tornadoes, to detect the exact nature of its corona, and to mark the precise instants of its partial or total obscuration, — the Sun of Righteousness, all unobserved, be dimmed and darkened in our own hearts, and an Eclipse of Faith be suffered to steal and settle over our land, whose beginning may be imperceptible, and its end beyond calculation?

Oh, let us hear and heed these warnings of the fathers to the children, as they come to us to-day, enforced not only by all the precious memories of their faith and piety, their virtues and sacrifices and sufferings, but by all the lessons and experiences of the times in which we live! We need not look beyond the events of the single year which is just closing, — this *Annus Mirabilis*, compared with which that of Dryden and Defoe was without significance or consequence; a year, more marvellous in its manifestations than almost any which has preceded it since the great year of our Lord, and from whose calendar no form of physical, political, or religious convulsion seems to have been wanting to startle and confound the nations; a year, whose Christmas, alas! is clouded and saddened by the continuance, in a land bound to us by memories not yet obliterated, of a conflict and a carnage which must fill every Christian heart with horror, and for the termination of which we would devoutly invoke the only Intervention which has not been, and which cannot be, rejected; — we need not, I say, look beyond the events of this single jubilee year of the Landing, to find evidence of the vanity of all human ambition and the impotence of all human power, and to see renewed and startling proof that while

> "A thousand years scarce serve to form a State,
> An hour may lay it in the dust."

Let us not be deaf to the warnings of the Fathers. Let us not be insensible to the lessons of the hour. Let us resolve that no National growth or grandeur, no civil freedom or social prosperity or individual success, shall ever render us unmindful of those great principles of piety and virtue which the Pilgrims inculcated and exemplified. Let us resolve that whatever else this nation shall be, or shall fail to be, it shall still and always be a Christian Nation, in the full comprehensiveness and true significance of that glorious term, — its example ever on the side of Peace and Justice; its eagle, not only with the shield of Union and Liberty emblazoned on its breast, but, like that of many a lectern of ancient cathedral or modern church, abroad or at home, ever proudly bearing up the open Bible on its outspread wings! And then, as year after year shall roll over our land, as jubilee shall succeed jubilee, and our children and our children's children shall gather on this consecrated spot to celebrate the event which has brought us here to-day, those grand closing words of Webster fifty years ago — the only words worthy to sum up the emotions of an hour like this, and send them down all sparkling and blazing to the remotest posterity, — shall be repeated and repeated by those who shall successively stand where he then stood, and where I stand now, not with any feeble expectation or faltering hope only, but with that firm persuasion, that undoubting confidence, that assured trust and faith, with which I adopt and repeat them as the closing words of another Jubilee discourse : —

"Advance, then, ye future generations! We would hail you, as you rise in your long succession to fill the places which we now fill, and to taste the blessings of existence where we are passing, and soon shall have passed, our own human duration. We bid you welcome to this pleasant land of the Fathers. We bid you welcome to the healthful skies and the verdant fields of New England. We greet your accession to the great inheritance which we have enjoyed. We welcome you to the blessings of good government and religious liberty. We welcome you to the treasures of science and the delights of learning. We welcome you to the transcendent sweets of domestic life, to the happiness of kindred and parents and children. We welcome you to the immeasurable blessings of rational existence, the immortal hope of Christianity, and the light of everlasting truth!"

NOTE.

(Page 57.)

The following inscription in the Hall of the Bishop of London's Palace, at Fulham, was copied for me most kindly by my venerable friend Bishop McIlvaine, of Ohio:—

"This Hall, with the adjoining quadrangle, was erected by Bishop Fitzjames in the reign of Henry VII. on the site of buildings of the old Palace as ancient as the Conquest. It was used as the Hall by Bishop Bonner and Bishop Ridley, during the struggles of the Reformation, and retained its original proportions till it was altered by Bishop Sherlock in the reign of George II. Bishop Howley, in the reign of George IV., changed it into a private unconsecrated Chapel. It is now restored to its original purpose on the erection by Bishop Tait of a new Chapel of more suitable dimensions.
"A. D. 1866."

The Palace must have been occupied by Richard Bancroft, during whose intolerant policy the Pilgrims fled to Holland; as he was Bishop of London for some years before becoming Archbishop of Canterbury. It must, also, have been occupied by Laud, from whose intolerance the Puritans suffered; as he, after serving as Bishop of St. David's, and of Bath and Wells, was translated to London in 1628, and continued in that See, exercising great influence over the ecclesiastical affairs of the realm, until he succeeded the more liberal Abbot as Primate of all England.

VI.

PRAYER.

By Rev. Joseph P. Thompson, D.D., of New York.

THINE, O Lord, is the greatness, and the power, and the glory, and the victory, and the majesty; for all that is in the heaven and in the earth is Thine. Thine is the kingdom, O Lord; and Thou art exalted as Head above all. Both riches and honor come of Thee; and in Thy hand it is to make great, and to give strength unto all. To Thee would we ascribe all praise and dominion, world without end.

We bless Thee that Thou hast given to Thy Son the kingdom upon earth; the kingdom of truth and holiness, of righteousness and grace; the kingdom of redeemed and sanctified souls, which shall outlast all the kingdoms of the world, and against which the gates of hell shall not prevail;—that Thou hast preserved Thy Church through conflicts with the powers of evil, through perils of persecution, and the more grievous perils of corruption and apostasy; that, in every age, Thou hast raised up faithful witnesses to Thy truth, the noble army of martyrs and confessors, who continually do praise Thee.

More especially do we this day bless Thee, the God of our Fathers, that when Reformation itself had need to be reformed, and Thy Church to be delivered from the powers of this world and the remnants of superstition, Thou didst search out by Thy Spirit the elect of Thine own kingdom, and didst call them to come out and be separate as the sons and daughters of the Lord Almighty; that they heard and obeyed Thy voice, and, trusting alone in Christ their Saviour and their Lord, committed their cause unto Him, in honoring His word and doing His will. For their faith and patience, their fidelity and devotion, their godly conversation, their loving care for their posterity, their great hope and inward zeal for the advancement of the gospel of the kingdom of Christ in these remote parts of the world, we render thanks to Thee, through Jesus Christ our Lord.

We bless Thee that Thou didst give unto them courage answerable to the great and honorable actions to which Thy providence did call them; — to fulfil all the Lord's ways, made known, or to be made known unto them, according to their best endeavors, whatever it might cost them, the Lord helping them. And we praise Thee that Thou didst help them to suffer all things for Christ's sake and the gospel's; to endure bonds and stripes and imprisonment, the spoiling of their goods, the loss of home, the privations of exile, the pains of death. O Thou great Head of the Church, who in Thine earthly ministry of love didst endure such contradiction of sinners against Thyself, we bless Thee that Thou didst strengthen these Thy servants with Thine own strength, and comfort them with Thy grace.

O Thou who leadest Joseph like a flock, whose way is in the sea, and Thy path in the great waters, we bless Thee that Thou didst guide our Fathers across the sea to these shores, didst here establish them in peace and safety, and through them establish thy Gospel in its simplicity, thy Church in its purity, and a Christian people, great and prosperous, as we are before Thee at this day.

Now therefore, O Lord, we beseech Thee, have respect unto Thy covenant, and incline our hearts to walk in the ways of our Fathers, as they followed Christ their Redeemer. Thou hast set in order before us our sins by the contrast of their godly lives; and we acknowledge our shortcomings, and confess with shame our unfaithfulness to Thy mercies, and to the goodly and blessed heritage unto which we have succeeded. O Lord, have mercy upon us still, and for Christ's sake pardon our iniquities; and grant, we beseech

Thee, that in this hour of hallowed and grateful memories, beneath these favoring skies, amid the tender and sacred associations of this scene, we may make it our purpose, by Thy grace, to serve Thee as our Fathers served Thee; to honor Thy Sabbath as they honored it; to obey Thy word as they obeyed it; to be ever true and firm for the right; to seek the glory of Thy Kingdom; and, like them, to set Christ above all, being rooted and grounded in Him as our life and salvation.

Almighty God who keepest covenant and mercy for them that love Thee, we bless Thee that Thy goodness to our Fathers hath been continued to their children from generation to generation; that Thou didst preserve our infant colonies, and bind them together in a union of States; didst carry them through the storm of war, and set them on high among the nations; and in our own time, when all that we as a People had received was brought into peril of destruction, Thou didst revive the spirit of the Pilgrims and their faith and hope in Thee, and inspire our sons and brothers to a like courage and sacrifice for the saving of the Nation. To Thy name, O LORD, be the glory, that freedom, order, and union are now established from sea to sea; that the land which in the beginning was a refuge from oppression no longer harbors oppression within its borders; and we pray Thee that the peoples gathered here from every land may be fused and moulded into one Brotherhood, dwelling in peace, seeking one another's good, and acknowledging one God and Father over all.

Bless all who are in authority: the Governor and Legislature of this Commonwealth, and all judges and magistrates; Thy servant the President of the United States, his counsellors, the Congress of the Nation, the Army and Navy, and all who are in places of power and trust throughout the land. Give unto them, we beseech Thee, wise counsels, and the spirit of justice and peace. Bless all schools of learning; and grant, we humbly pray Thee, that these may ever be consecrated as at the first to Christ and His Church.

We supplicate Thy favor upon this ancient Church and town, praying that the faith and spirit of the Fathers may here abide in their children. Bless Thy holy Church universal, and fill her with Thy light and love. O LORD, save Thy people, and bless Thine heritage; govern them and lift them up for ever.

Thou Prince of Peace, who art Head over all things to Thy Church, we beseech Thee hasten the return of peace among the nations; and from all the commotions and terrors of this present time bring forth anew the beauty and order of Thy kingdom. Have compassion, O LORD, upon the wounded and dying, the sick and the prisoner, and upon all whose hearts and homes are made desolate by war; and bring on the blessed day when the nations shall learn war no more. So, through the ages to come, may the truths and the actions which we have in remembrance this day exert their power for the recovery of mankind unto that true life and liberty which are in Jesus Christ our Lord. Keep us, O LORD, ever mindful of the lessons of this day. May we carry them with us to our homes; may we teach them to our children; may we preserve them as a guide and help in all our pilgrimage, till by Thy grace we too shall come unto the spirits of just men made perfect, to the general assembly and Church of the first-born in the Jerusalem that is above; through Jesus Christ our Lord.

Our Father which art in heaven, Hallowed be Thy name. Thy kingdom come. Thy will be done in earth, as it is in heaven. Give us this day our daily bread. Forgive us our trespasses, as we forgive them that trespass against us. And lead us not into temptation, but deliver us from evil. For Thine is the Kingdom, and the Power, and the Glory, for ever. *Amen.*

VII.

HYMN.

Composed by WILLIAM CULLEN BRYANT, of New York; read by Rev. T. E. ST. JOHN, of Worcester; and sung by the Choir to the tune of "Old Hundred," with Orchestral Accompaniment.

> WILD was the day, the wintry sea
>   Moaned sadly on New England's strand,
> When first, the thoughtful and the free,
>   Our Fathers trod the desert land.
>
> They little thought how pure a light,
>   With years, should gather round that day!
> How love should keep their memories bright!
>   How wide a realm their sons should sway!
>
> Green are their bays; and greener still
>   Shall round their spreading fame be wreathed;
> And regions now untrod shall thrill
>   With reverence when their names are breathed;
>
> Till where the sun, with softer fires,
>   Looks on the vast Pacific's sleep,
> The children of the Pilgrim sires
>   This hallow'd day like us shall keep.

VIII.

BENEDICTION.

By REV. FREDERIC N. KNAPP.

"May the grace of our Lord Jesus Christ, the love of God our Father, and the fellowship of His Holy Spirit, be and abide with you now and for ever. *Amen.*"

IX.

VOLUNTARY.

Selections from "Il Trovatore," by Gilmore's Band.

THE DINNER.

AT the conclusion of the exercises in the church the procession at once re-formed, and marched to the railway station, where the dinner took place. The station-house had been closed in, the tracks floored over, the hall thoroughly heated and neatly decorated, and every preparation made for lighting it. Plates were laid for nine hundred persons, and every seat was occupied. Ladies to the number of about three hundred had been admitted, in accordance with the plans of the Committee, and were seated at the tables when the procession arrived. At the centre of the guests' table three ancient chairs were placed, all of which were brought over in the "Mayflower," and were owned by Governor Carver and Elder Brewster and Governor Bradford. The first two belong to the Pilgrim Society, and the last to NATHANIEL RUSSELL, Esq., of Plymouth. These were occupied by the Presiding Officer, the Orator of the Day, and the President of the Society. The tables were arranged with care and taste, and loaded with well-selected, well-cooked, and well-served viands, reflecting much credit on Mr. Field, the caterer, who performed the service required of him under his contract in a manner entirely satisfactory to the Committee.[6] Five kernels of parched corn were placed at each plate, to illustrate the extremity to which the Pilgrims were at one time reduced.[7]

At about half-past three o'clock all were seated, when Hon. WILLIAM T. DAVIS, of Plymouth, rose and said, —

At the request of the Hon. EDWARD S. TOBEY, President of the Pilgrim Society, who will be unable to remain during the dinner, I, as Vice-President of the Society and Chairman of the Committee of Arrangements, take the chair, and shall preside over this festival.

You will now listen to a blessing from the Rev. HENRY M. DEXTER, D.D., of Boston.

PRAYER BY REV. DR. DEXTER.

Almighty God, who didst give our Fathers grace to thank Thee for the treasures hid in the sand, and by their faith and with unconquerable will to serve Thee in their narrow circumstances, grant unto us, their children, we beseech Thee, grace to thank Thee for Thy goodness to us, through them, and for Thy goodness to us in all things; and help us to so use our advantages and privileges in Thy service, that we may be accepted of Thee, as they were; for Christ's sake. *Amen.*

A pleasant hour was spent in relieving the tables of their load, at the expiration of which the President called the company to order, and addressed them as follows: —

SPEECH OF HON. WILLIAM T. DAVIS.

Sons and Daughters of the Pilgrims! — Why are you gathered here to-day? What has brought you from your homes, under a winter sky, to this bleak New England coast? No summer landscape greets your eyes: the cold billows of the Atlantic roll and throw their spray along the shore. No gentle breezes from the verdant hills fan your heated brows: the chill northern blast sweeps sadly through the branches of our leafless woods. What charmed word has gone, like Scotland's fiery cross, over hills and plains to summon you to this spot? No battle-field of the war, with its silent graves and sacred memories, stretches out before your feet, calling you to a new consecration to your country and your flag; no monument to the immortal dead rears its shaft aloft, awaiting its dedication at your hands.

No battle-field did I say? Ah! more sacred than any which ancient or modern history records is the battle-field on which you have this day trod. Agincourt, Austerlitz, Cannæ, Marathon, Thermopylæ, stamped as they are on the historic page as among the decisive battles of the world, sink into insignificance beside the battle which our Fathers fought along the hill-sides and round the Rock of Plymouth. No armed hosts with shining helmet and waving plume met here in battle array; no trumpet sounded the charge; no warrior's lance or bristling steel met the opposing foe; no royal hand crowned the victorious chief. No new division of regal power, no readjustment of imperial lines, no fate of potentate or prince, depended on the issue. But in that battle a new civilization asserted its claim against the insolent pretensions of the old; the rights of man stood up against the domination of kings; the human conscience fought to free itself from the shackles of servitude. This was the battle which our Fathers fought; and neither hunger nor hardship, nor the terrible uncertainties of the future, nor the allurements of their distant home, nor pestilence nor death, could check their courage or shake their faith. With the battle still raging, ay, well-nigh lost; with one-half their number sleeping in their graves, — as if to stimulate a trust which they feared might fade, they sent their only refuge back across the seas, and sought with a serener confidence the guidance and protection of their God.

Historians record and poets sing that the Saracens of old destroyed their ships when they landed for conquest on the coast of Spain. But those Moslem hosts had stood on the shores of Africa flushed with victory, sighing for new lands to conquer, and they knew their arms were invincible. A brighter page and a sweeter song shall proclaim to nations yet unborn, as the noblest typification of faith in God, that sublimer incident in Christian history, the return of the "Mayflower" to England.[8]

Welcome, sons and daughters of the Pilgrims, to this hallowed field. Kneel reverently over the graves of your fathers, and swear anew your allegiance to their cause. Inhale, with fullest breath, the atmosphere of this sacred spot; drink long and deep at this fountain of our Nation's greatness. Go back to your homes with no boast of your lineage on your lips, but with the vow recorded in your hearts to make yourselves worthier descendants of a noble ancestry. There are monumental acts as well as monumental edifices; and even when the memorial on yonder hill shall in the fulness of time be completely finished, and its finger of faith shall point upward to the skies, let us remember that fidelity to duty — duty to ourselves, our country, and our God — will be the noblest monument which the children can rear in memory of the virtues and sacrifices of the Pilgrim Fathers of New England.

The PRESIDENT. — I propose, as the first regular sentiment, —

The Pilgrims of 1620 : Weak, despised, exiled, they conquered a continent: they are revolutionizing the world.

I call upon Hon. EDWARD S. TOBEY, President of the Pilgrim Society, to respond.

SPEECH OF HON. E. S. TOBEY.

Mr. President, Ladies and Gentlemen, — To respond to the toast which has been given in honor of men of whom it has been justly said "the world was not worthy" is no ordinary task; and I might well wish, on your account, if not on my own, that some more gifted descendant of the Pilgrims had been selected for this duty.

We have listened to-day to the eloquent words of one of Massachusetts' most gifted sons, a lineal descendant of the honored Governor Winthrop, as he has sketched the historic picture to which he has left little to be added by those who are now gathered around this festive board. It may be said, however, with all deference to him, that the subject is too vast for any one person, on any one occasion, to entertain even a hope of completing it. We may repeat — indeed, we cannot fail to repeat — many of the principles and thoughts which have been so vividly brought before us to-day. I have intimated that the "master hand" has left some portions of the picture not quite complete. The sentiment just proposed has devolved on me the humble task of adding some of the lighter shades by which the prominent features he has so boldly sketched may stand out in still stronger relief. If I shall succeed in performing even that subordinate part, as I shall imperfectly and very briefly refer to the more recent as well as the possible future history of our country as related to the principles of the Pilgrim Fathers, I may not wholly fail to meet the demands of the occasion.

Two centuries and a half have rolled away since our Fathers placed their feet on yonder hallowed Rock; and we have gathered from every part of our land around this ancestral family altar, to lay on it the tribute of grateful hearts. Indeed, what more can we do to-day? Words are often inadequate; they are transient. Deeds are immortal. May we not well point to the heroic deeds of the sons of the Pilgrims, in defence of the Union, as some evidence of their gratitude, and that they both honor and appreciate the principles which lie at the foundation of this Republic? We have with us to-day, I rejoice to see, descendants of the Pilgrims, who fought on many a bloody field, and have thus repeated the sacrifice of the Fathers. On my left is one of the distinguished heroes of Gettysburg, who rolled back the tide of rebellion, until the Union flag floated victoriously on those memorable heights, now for ever made historic. Says my informant, "I asked one of the aids of General Lee to what he attributed the loss of the battle of Gettysburg. 'Why,' said he, ' we expected victory as much as we expected to go there, but every plan we laid was contravened from morning till night; and I believe that if ever God deserted our cause, it was there.'" Yes, my friends, he did desert it; indeed, he never was with it. But he was with the descendants of the Pilgrims there, in the persons of those who carried the Union army to victory. Yes: the God of our Fathers *was with them;* and then and there the tide of rebellion was stayed, the national government delivered from the hands of its enemies, and the American Union, let us hope, for ever established.

Now what remains for this Nation is to go forward and consummate this work through the oft-recognized but indispensable agencies, — the open Bible, the school-house, the meeting-house, and, last but not least, through that without which even the Bible, if I may say it reverently, must be restricted in its influence, — the free ballot. The ballot must be maintained and defended at any and all costs. I believe that every patriotic heart in this land felt a deeper thrill when it was known that he who once carried our arms to victory, the President of the United States, had the courage to say by the presence of national troops in the city of New York, as he doubtless will say throughout the country, "The ballot-box must and shall be protected."

With such institutions and measures let this Nation go forward. Let us fear no emigration from the one side or the other. This country is emphatically the asylum for the oppressed of all nations·

Welcome them on either shore, the Atlantic or the Pacific. If our Fathers, in the wilderness and amidst savages, could afford to trust in their Bible and in the living God, — if the missionary could plant the standard of the cross in the Sandwich Islands, trusting in the God of our Fathers, until those islands, converted to Christianity, now, like gems in mid ocean, flash the rays of Christian civilization over the world, — cannot their descendants, with the vast moral resources and constantly augmenting power of this Nation, and a faith resting on the same enduring foundations, discharge the responsible trust bequeathed to them, of transmitting to posterity, and to the people of all nations who are seeking a home here, the institutions of civil and religious freedom? America is indeed destined to be the educator of the world. Instead of relying on missionary efforts alone, invaluable as they have been and are, to Christianize the idolatrous nations, many circumstances conspire to bring the people of foreign lands to our shores in ever-increasing numbers, to be moulded to Christianity through the influence of our institutions as well as by direct teachings of the Gospel. Accepting the responsibilities of the hour which Providence has placed on this Nation let it ever continue in the fulfilment of its great mission. Thus will it best testify its gratitude to the founders of the Republic, and may confidently hope for the continued blessing of Almighty God. Then shall it literally inherit the divine promise: " I will give the heathen for an inheritance and the uttermost parts of the earth for a possession."

The PRESIDENT. — I have received by telegraph the following toast from the President of the United States : —

Our Pilgrim Fathers: May their children ever be as pure in motive, as patient in toil, and as brave in danger.

The PRESIDENT. — In reply to that sentiment, I will give the following toast : —

The President of the United States: The representative of forty millions of freemen, sheltered by the branches of the tree which our Fathers planted.

Hon. THOMAS RUSSELL will respond.

SPEECH OF HON. THOMAS RUSSELL.

The name of the President, the words of the President, move all hearts. As his message unites Washington with Plymouth, so the magic of eloquence to-day has brought 1870 and 1620 into full accord. The sentiment suggests a wonderful contrast: Governor Carver, with his hundred shivering exiles, and President Grant, ruler of forty millions of free men, — of a land greater in ideas and principles of government than in degrees of longitude and latitude. We turn from the poor, lonely "Mayflower," with timbers strained and rigging torn, staggering into Cape Cod harbor, to our mighty fleet sweeping up the Mississippi or into Mobile Bay, guided by that heart of oak, our good and gallant Farragut. We contrast Miles Standish leading his half score of soldiers to Middleboro' or Weymouth, with Sherman marching from the mountains to the sea; with Grant laying hold of Vicksburg and crushing rebellion at Appomattox. And we love to believe that all the glory of these days was prefigured in the faith of the days of old. The grim jest of our Fathers named "Billington Sea" in remembrance of the wanderer who mistook it for the Pacific. Yet might some graver pilgrim, as he stood upon the Burial Hill, their mount of vision, have seen afar off a country stretching from ocean to ocean, as he cried out in prophecy —

"From Eastern rock to sunset sea
The Continent is ours."

I find strong points of resemblance in the great hearts of these distant ages. Look at the Indian policy of our Fathers, — justice and humanity, equality between the races; the unbroken treaty made on the hill beyond the brook; peace secured by right. Two hundred and fifty years have passed away. Once more the red man is treated like a man; and once more the world learns that the truest policy is justice. Honor to the Pilgrims; honor to him who renews their noble policy. I find a broader resemblance in the firm, the obstinate devotion to duty which marks the hero of each age. Often might General Grant and his associates have exclaimed: "It is not with us as with men whom small things discourage." Just here our Fathers fought out their battle of the wilderness. And they were determined to fight it out on the line of right and faith, though it took them ten winters before they were reinforced by another colony. Grander still is the identity of principle. In a dark hour, when the only light for Union shone round the bayonets of the Army of the South-West, General Grant uttered this noble sentiment: "Human freedom, the only true foundation for human government." This idea embodied in action gave us victory. This was our Fathers' creed. Freedom from human control in matters of faith — sure to result in freedom of State — was their guide. Grand is the compact of the "Mayflower;" but many such a compact bound together the scattered churches of the free. To-day is kept sacred by a great sect, eminent in ability and piety, who celebrate the birth of Congregationalism in America. They might have chosen a broader word; they might have boasted of a greater triumph. Independency — yes, Democracy in the name of Independency — stood on the sacred Rock, and claimed the continent for its own. Because Independents, our Fathers were tolerant, free, fitted to found a free State on a free Church. We honor the Puritans of Old England and New England, as we honor the grand old Church out of which the Puritan rock was hewed; but we cannot forget that no Puritan came in the "Mayflower." Independents and Separatists, all of them, every man of prominence, except Miles Standish, who belonged to no church, except the church of those whose creed is to strike down wrong, and to uphold the weak. As I speak of Captain Standish, I love to recall the fact that the same arm which smote to death the savage Pecksuot was tenderly folded around sick men and dying women and famishing children, — glorious symbol of the Nation, that with one hand smote armed rebellion, while the other raised up a poor, despised, oppressed race, that they might take the place for which God sent them into the world. And this last triumph of right we owe to Pilgrim principles. All that series of victories, beginning with the Declaration of Independence and ending (no, not ending) with the declaration of the equality of man, — they were all assured, they were all DECREED, when a new world became the possession of a band of earnest men, whose faith was that in the chief concern of man he had no superior, save his Maker. Once the Mayflower of the woods was the emblem of our country, — the Mayflower, shrinking from the cold, hiding under the leaves, only enduring the frost in the faith of approaching spring. Now she is likened to the spreading cedar, to the proud oak, — better far, as the Orator of to-day has said, our nation is as the tree of life, whose leaves are for the healing of the nations, — yes, at last, of all nations. It is our faith that even the wickedness of war, the crimes of Emperors, the madness of Kings, shall turn the hearts of men to the lessons of Plymouth Rock, to the example of the American Union.

> "Take, Freedom! take thy radiant round:
> When dimmed, revive; when lost, return;
> Till not a shrine on earth be found
> Whereon thy glories shall not burn."

The PRESIDENT then announced the next regular toast, as follows: —

Plymouth and Jamestown — the Pilgrims and the Cavaliers — Freedom and Slavery: They met on the field of Gettysburg, and Freedom conquered.

The PRESIDENT. — General HOWARD, the hero of Gettysburg.

SPEECH OF GEN. O. O. HOWARD.

I thank you, Mr. President, and the other gentlemen who have been instrumental in inviting me to be present on this occasion. I have really been to-day a learner, and from my entrance into the town of Plymouth until this moment I have been enjoying a perpetual feast. I thank you again for the sentiment which a few moments ago I read for the first time. It really is the embodiment of a speech. It needs very little to elaborate it. Plymouth and the Pilgrims on one side, Jamestown and the Cavaliers on the other, — the conflict which Mr. Seward called "irrepressible" between Freedom and Slavery. We have only to congratulate ourselves to-day that slavery is no more. You will notice in that little compact which was made before the Pilgrims landed, that the first sentiment, — a sentiment which is to-day repeated in every document, and quoted in every speech that is made in regard to them, — the first sentiment was "the honor and glory of God." That they put first and foremost; and I thank the Orator of the Day with all my soul for his fidelity, that he kept prominently before us, from the beginning to the end of his discourse, the fundamental sentiment of those men, our Fathers, who came to this country, to suffer, to toil, and to die, that they might perpetuate the principles they held so dear and sacred. I would that we might to-day stop and think and pray, and go back to that original principle of holding up before all things else the God of our Fathers, and the Lord Jesus Christ as His express image. If we would only be loyal to Him, first and foremost, then indeed and in truth would the great object of the conflict to which I have referred be, not only seemingly, but in reality accomplished.

But it seems to me, as we listen to this history, as we reflect upon the situation to-day, and as we congratulate ourselves upon what has already been accomplished, we should do well, as our Orator has told us, to stop and consider our shortcomings, consider our errors, and consider how we have departed from the pure and simple principles of our Fathers, in so many ways; and to begin anew, to repent, to turn back unto God, become loyal to His Son, our Saviour, and go forth into the field of conflict again, and fight until the end of our existence, and sow seed that shall spring up and bear fruit for generations to come.

What is this conflict, and where are the fields on which it is to be fought? They are at home; they are in our families; they are in our churches; they are in our towns, of which this town of Plymouth is a representative; they are throughout our borders. The fields are wherever the foreigners who come among us are to be found; they are where the Indians are to-day; they are where the Chinese are. Let us go forth, and carry the banner of the cross wherever we go, and fearlessly plant ourselves on the simple faith of the simple and true church of the Pilgrims. God grant that all the descendants of the Pilgrims, and all who love their pure principles, who are here present to-day, may be prepared to make a sacrifice of themselves for the good of their fellow-men, that they may establish for ever in their own households, in the community, in the State, in these blessed United States, and in the world, that principle which is above every other principle, which is expressed in these words, that are inimitable: "Thou shalt love the Lord thy God with all thy heart, and thy neighbor as thyself." Let that neighbor be of any race, whether it be African or Anglo-Saxon, whether it be Indian or Chinese; from whatever region of the world he may come. God grant that we may be brave enough and pure enough to carry this leaven with us wherever we go. And may the time soon come when this Nation shall be a purified people, purified unto the Lord our God, and when we shall be in deed and in truth a missionary nation, to carry peace and good-will wherever we go, and to carry the blessed Gospel into every part of the known world.

I am a soldier. I have endeavored to fight your battles on many a field, of which Gettysburg has been referred to as a type; but I tell you the true conflict is that of true Christian men and true Christian women.

The PRESIDENT here stated, in order that visitors from abroad might feel perfectly easy with regard to the departure of trains, that arrangements had been made for an express and way train to Boston, after the dinner, and that he should give thirty minutes' notice of the time of their departure.

He then recalled to mind the fact, that in October, 1632, John Winthrop, the Governor of the Colony of Massachusetts, in order to cultivate friendship with the Pilgrims, made an excursion to Plymouth, and was two days on his way. He followed the Indian trail through Scituate, Hanover, Pembroke, and Kingston, and was received outside of the town by Governor Bradford. He remained in Plymouth over Sunday, and, as the tradition states, "spoke in meeting." The President closed these prefatory remarks by announcing as the next regular toast, [9] —

The Orator of the Day: As his Puritan ancestor followed the trail of the Indians to speak words of friendship to the Pilgrims, so he to-day has followed the trail of his ancestor, and spoken words of wisdom and eloquence to their descendants.

SPEECH OF HON. ROBERT C. WINTHROP.

Mr. President, Ladies and Gentlemen, — I am sure the whole company will agree with me in one thing, at least; and that is that my voice has been heard for a sufficient time already on this occasion. I propose, therefore, in a very few words to make my acknowledgments to you all for this kind and friendly greeting, and for the compliment expressed in the sentiment just offered. I hope I may be allowed to take it as the welcome assurance that I have not altogether disappointed my audience in the effort I have made to-day. You know, Mr. President, that it was with no little distrust and hesitation that I accepted the flattering invitation of your Committee. I could not forget whom I was to follow. That man encounters no easy or enviable responsibility who attempts to glean a field over which have already successively passed the broad scythe of Daniel Webster and the golden sickle of Edward Everett. I am conscious of having followed them *longo intervallo,* in more senses of the words than one. I might, indeed, claim to have been at least one day ahead of them both; since we of this generation have learned that we are not quite so far behind our Fathers as we thought we were, and that the 21st and not the 22d of December, which they celebrated, is the true date of the landing. But I confess to being a full half century behind at least one of them in every other respect. I was hardly of an age to be here with Webster fifty years ago. At any rate, I was not here. But I well remember how the fame of that oration shook every school-bench in New England, and how soon it supplied the choicest pieces of declamation for every school-boy. Four years afterward I was here; and I shall not soon forget that long, wintry stage-coach drive of ten or twelve hours each way, in company, I am glad to remember, with one of your own townsmen, who has long since been at the head of our Boston Bar (Hon. Sidney Bartlett), and in company too, I believe, — for certainly we were here together, — with the excellent pastor of our Boston Brattle Street Church (Rev. Dr. Lothrop). But still less can I forget how abundantly and superabundantly we were all rewarded for the fatigues and exposures of our journey by the magnificent oration of Edward Everett.

May I be pardoned, however, for adding that it was not only the vivid remembrance of what others had done here so gloriously which made me shrink from undertaking the task you assigned me? May I be pardoned for confessing that I was a little afraid of my own shadow? I could not quite forget that in the city of New York, at the call of the New England Society there, I had gone over the same ground thirty-one years ago to-morrow. I was then but half as old as I am now, and had all the energy and ambition of youth. It was my very first Occasional Address anywhere, I believe; and I had spared no pains in its preparation. It was two hours and ten minutes in delivery; and I remember that at the end my cherished and lamented friend, the late Bishop Wainwright, who had sat near me, called my attention to the fact, of which I had been entirely unconscious, that my manuscript had been upside down during the whole time. I should not dare to trust my memory with such a load in these later years of my life. And, indeed, I despaired of being able to compose another address on the same subject half as good as that was; and I am by no means sure that I have done so. But while I was pondering upon these and other discouragements and difficulties, I suddenly bethought me of that old Massachusetts Colony, with which you have so kindly associated me. I bethought me what a comfort, what a delight, it must have been to them on their arrival at Salem, in the first desolation of their condition, not only to find Endicott and Higginson on the spot awaiting them; but to know that Bradford and Brewster and Winslow were already established here at Plymouth, ready and eager to exchange, as they did exchange, the right hand of fellowship with them.[10] I bethought me of that noble first Governor (John Winthrop), whose blood to-day seems coursing through my veins in a fuller tide than ever before, and whose image seemed to rebuke me for hesitating an instant to speak in his name, as well as in my own, in honor of the Pilgrims. He reminded me of the powder which he had himself furnished them, in a time of their distress and danger, at his own cost, and how gratefully it was received and acknowledged by them. And so, Mr. President, while I was musing, the fire burned, and I resolved to speak with my tongue, as I have spoken to-day. I resolved, in a word, that I would not decline to supply to the descendants of the Pilgrims, for their occasion and at their call, such ammunition as I could muster, even should it be at my own cost; — feeling sure that they would make all proper allowances for the fact that others had already exhausted the essential ingredient for such a composition, — that Attic salt, which is as necessary for an oration as saltpetre is for gunpowder.[11]

But I have occupied far more of the time of this occasion than belongs to me; and I must not delay you longer, while so many others remain to be called on. Let me only say that as the Pilgrims gave me the earliest inspiration in the way of occasional oratory, I shall be more than content if they shall have afforded me the last. If I have had any faculty in dealing with such occasions as this, — and I am sensible how small it is, — I am ready to say to-day at Plymouth Rock, "*Hic cestus artemque repono.*" I can certainly say that I shall be present in the body at no other Pilgrim Jubilee. Let me only hasten, then, to thank you and your Society, and all who have so kindly listened to me, for the distinguished compliment which has been paid me, and let me propose as a sentiment, —

The Sons and Daughters of New England: Wherever they may be gathered, and wherever they may be scattered, here and in every clime, now and to the end of time, may they never forget the Rock, nor ever fail to be true to the memory and the example of those who landed upon it.

The PRESIDENT. — I will read as the next sentiment: —

The distinguished Son of the Orator of 1824: More fortunate than his father in tracing his descent from the Pilgrims.

I will introduce to you WILLIAM EVERETT, Esq.

POEM BY WILLIAM EVERETT, ESQ.

Ladies and Gentlemen, — I was requested a short time ago by the Chairman to furnish something in verse for this occasion; and as I was not wholly averse to writing verse, I trust it will not prove that I am perverse, and that my effort is not entirely a reverse. If I can have your attention for seventy lines only, I shall be content.

PLYMOUTH ROCK — 1620 — 1870.

Strike up the good old song once more, upon the good old day;
The good old blood has reason yet the good old words to say:
They've pressed us hard, these modern men, and blustered loud and
    long,
To drown the ancient echoes of that good old Pilgrim song.
Now since the Lord has sent again the year of Jubilee,
Here comes our challenge, scoffers, to ring from sea to sea:
There's nothing this new world can show to beat the good old stock,
The vine the Fathers planted this day on Plymouth Rock!

You boys of rail and telegraph, say, whence did you derive
Your energy to trample, your genius to contrive?
Could you have borne an ocean voyage as patiently as they,
From August to December, with sermons twice a day?
Your wonderful inventions, — say, have you got the skill
To make the Mayflower furniture, that multiplies at will, —
The Edward Winslow tables, the William Bradford clock,
The Richard Warren high-backed chairs, all dumped on Plymouth Rock?

You're great on Agriculture; it's arduous work to till
Those broad, fat river bottoms, on which you sit so still.
A stubborn land, a stormy sea, they fought with spade and rod,
And found the chief productions were granite and salt cod.
Your population's spreading; with them was it begun,
One child born on the ocean, and in the harbor one.
And never did the Lord vouchsafe his increase to his flock
Richer than to the five-score souls that stepped on Plymouth Rock.

Your boasted institutions, your colleges and schools
To teach the whole world every thing, yet leave us still some fools;
Your companies that turn to stock all things beneath the sun,
And read our Nation's motto, "The many *lost* in one;"
Your leagues and constitutions spread like net-work o'er the land, —
Are feeble to the cords of steel that bound the Pilgrim band.
And in itself one compact doth all their treasures lock,
Signed in the "Mayflower's" cabin, and sealed on Plymouth Rock.

That liberty you proudly claim of action and of thought
Was all across the ocean by Scrooby's Pilgrims brought;
A harder need compelled them to leave a peaceful home;
They found a fiercer savage within these forests roam.
So in your honest triumph beware how ye withhold
Due honor from your Fathers, the mighty men of old.
At home they met unflinching the cell, the scourge, the block,
And here the land's foundations laid firm on Plymouth Rock.

We know the fun you love so well at Puritans to poke,
Your witches and your Quakers and every threadbare joke.
Go read your history, school-boys; learn on one glorious page
The Pilgrim towers untainted above that iron age.
From stains of mightiest heroes the Pilgrims' hands are clean,
In Plymouth's free and peaceful streets no bigot's stake was seen;
The sons of other saints may wince and pale beneath your mock,
Harmless the fool-born jesting flows back from Plymouth Rock.

Nay, let the strain soar higher; still louder swell the song;
Claim all the starry honors that to our sires belong;
Two hundred years and fifty, brothers, this day have flown,
Since first from out the godless world our Fathers came alone.
Then France was flown with glory, and Spain was swol'n with pride,
And England rested in her might, and Rome the world defied:
The scoff of sword and sceptre, of mitre and of frock,
The seed of God in tears was sown this day on Plymouth Rock.

One-fourth of time's great cycle hath o'er the ages passed,
And the stroke of God's great vengeance the guilty finds at last.
Helpless the Roman tyrant is shaking on his hill,
And Spain before a stranger boy must bend her haughty will!
The plains of France are trampled in gore by steel-hoofed foes,
And England hears a warning in every breeze that blows;
At all the godless thresholds Death's equal footsteps knock,
But peace and joy and safety are ours on Plymouth Rock.

The storm of God's destruction is sweeping o'er the skies,
The rains in wrath are falling, the floods in anger rise ;
Woe to the men who on the race he loves have laid their hand,
And woe to all the foolish ones who build upon the sand.
Let torrents fall and billows swell, and winds their fury spend :
Our Fathers' God from every ill their children shall defend.
No cloud can dim our nation's sun, no stroke our dwelling shock,
By great Jehovah founded this day on Plymouth Rock.

The PRESIDENT. — I have received by telegraph the following toast from the New England Society of St. Louis : —

Plymouth Rock: The foundation-stone of Western civilization.

In response to which, I will propose —

The Great West: The cap-stone of the monument which shall stand in everlasting memory of the Pilgrim Fathers of New England.

The PRESIDENT. — The next toast which I will propose is as follows : —

The Compact of the Mayflower: [12] The first written constitution the world ever saw, the foundation-stone of free governments, "the first effectual counterpoise in the scale of human rights."

The PRESIDENT called on Hon. HENRY WILSON to respond, who was heartily greeted.

SPEECH OF HON. HENRY WILSON.

These flying moments admonish me that I must make but a brief response to the sentiment just given by the chair, and so kindly received. The Orator of the Day, in the magnificent address to which we have listened with high gratification, — an address which honors him alike as a scholar, as an orator, as a statesman, and as a Christian, — has told us that it was the Christian faith that brought the Pilgrims, who stepped on Plymouth Rock two hundred and fifty years ago this day, to the Western world. While I agree in the sentiment that it was piety, pure and simple faith in God and in his Son, that brought those brave men across the waves, I cannot forget — we should all gratefully remember on this day — that they laid in the cabin of the "Mayflower" the foundations of civil liberty in America. Bancroft, in his history, tells us that in the cabin of the "Mayflower" humanity recovered its rights; that government was then founded by them on the basis of equal law for the general good. That compact proclaimed that, for the glory of God, the advancement of the Christian faith, the honor of country, the general good, there should be just and equal laws. These grand doctrines of the Pilgrims, then embodied in a compact of government, have been inspirations and examples in all the succeeding generations. From the day that compact was signed to the time in which we live, there has been a struggle here in the Western world to establish and maintain just and equal laws for the general good. The example of the Pilgrims has inspired the faith and strengthened the arms of those who have battled in legislative halls and on bloody fields. It inspired the colonies in their struggle for more than a century against the aggressive policy of England. It inspired the burning eloquence of James Otis, and the pen of the organizer of the American Revolution, that grand old Puritan, Samuel Adams. It inspired the majestic eloquence of Daniel Webster, when he stood here half a century ago, and denounced the slave-trade as the crime of his century. It inspired John Quincy Adams in his grand struggle, in the hall of Congress, to maintain the sacred right of petition; and the martyred Lovejoy to vindicate, on the banks of the Mississippi, the freedom of the press. It inspired William Lloyd Garrison when he proclaimed immediate emancipation and his firm resolve to be heard by the American people. It inspired Abraham Lincoln in his immortal Proclamation of Emancipation, which smote the fetters from the limbs of three and a half millions of men. It inspired brave men among the living and the dead, in minorities and in majorities, in the long struggle which incorporated into the Constitution the thirteenth amendment, that made it impossible that a slave should tread the soil of the Republic; the fourteenth amendment, that defined the rights of American citizenship; and the fifteenth amendment, that gave every male citizen the right to vote, and practically the right to be voted for. This grand compact of government on board the "Mayflower," adopted before the men who made it had trod the soil of the continent, will inspire their descendants and brave men in the advancing future to hope on and struggle on to make equal and just laws for the general good, the vital, animating, and living spirit of American institutions, so long as the memory of the Pilgrims shall live in the Western world.

The President. — The next sentiment which I proposed to offer was to be responded to by a gentleman who is necessarily absent. I cannot forbear, however, giving the toast in honor of our absent guest, WILLIAM LLOYD GARRISON, Esq, —

The great Captains of Freedom, who gracefully surrendered their commissions when the victory was won.

I have a letter, received to day from Mr. Garrison, in which he expresses regret at not being able to be present, and adds in a postscript: "If I were present at your commemorative dinner, I could offer no sentiment more in accordance with my own mind, or more appropriate to the occasion, than is contained in the following lines by Lowell: —

" 'New occasions teach new duties; time makes ancient good uncouth;
They must upward still and onward, who would keep abreast of Truth.
Lo! before us gleam her camp-fires! we ourselves must Pilgrims be;
Launch our Mayflower, and steer boldly through the desperate winter sea,
Nor attempt the Future's portal with the Past's blood-rusted key.'"

The President. — The next sentiment which I have to propose is as follows: —

The past Orators of this Anniversary: They have added lustre to a day already famous in the annals of our history.

I introduce to you the Hon. GEORGE S. HILLARD, of Boston.

SPEECH OF HON. GEORGE S. HILLARD.

In asking me to speak to this toast, you set me a task embarrassing from the very wealth of matter which the theme presents. The first and the second and the third virtue of an after-dinner speech is that it shall be short; and I could not do justice to the past orators of this occasion without speaking at such length as to break this rule, and make you all wish that I too were a past and not a present orator.

The landing of the Pilgrims was not publicly noticed until long after the last survivor of them had been gathered to his fathers. Like many memorable events in history, its significance was not revealed to the actors. In nothing were the Pilgrim Fathers more admirable than in their unconsciousness and absolute freedom from self-reference. Like Moses when he came down from Mount Sinai, with the tablets of testimony in his hand, they wist not that their faces shone. It is ever thus with spiritual light. It is a glory not perceived by him upon whom it rests; and the moment a man knows that his face shines, that moment the light begins to grow dim.

The first public celebration took place so late as 1769, and was under the auspices of a club of Plymouth gentlemen, among whom we see the still familiar names of Watson, Warren, Davis, and Russell. It was attended with such expressions and marks of honor as were at command in those days of plain living and modest means. A cannon was fired, a flag was raised, a procession was formed, and a "decent repast" was served, beginning with a large baked Indian whortleberry pudding. This was in conformity with the good old New England usage, which was to serve pudding first. Perhaps this reversal of the natural order of dinner was due to the reverence felt by our Fathers for the primitive language of the Old Testament, since in the Hebrew Bible the beginning of the book is at the end of the volume. In the evening there was a social gathering at the Old Colony Hall, where the President of the club "delivered several appropriate toasts." Whether these toasts were dry or dipped, we are not informed.

The next year, 1770, just a hundred years ago to-morrow, the day was celebrated in much the same manner as in the preceding year, with the addition of an address, which was spoken "with decent firmness," by Edward Winslow, Jr., Esq., a member of the club; and, as his discourse was not above ten minutes in length, the firmness of the hearers could not have been severely tried.

During the remainder of the second century, except during the thirteen years between 1780 and 1794, the event was noticed by either a public or a private celebration, and discourses were delivered by men of note; among them John Quincy Adams, President Kirkland, Horace Holley, and Francis C. Gray, — the last a remarkable man, but who has left little behind him to show what cause his friends had to admire his abilities and attainments.

But you, Mr. President, will permit me to pause for a moment upon one name in the list of early orators, that of Judge Davis, your kinsman, who gave the discourse in 1800. No man was better fitted to speak on this theme; for no one had studied the lives and labors of the Pilgrims more carefully, and no one felt for them a deeper reverence. His was the pure and lofty spirit of the Pilgrims, softened by the influences of a milder age and a creed less stern. In him were seen the "*prisca fides*," the ancestral faith of Marcellus, and the "*mitis sapientia*," the gentle wisdom of Lælius. He was wise and good, tender and true: the calm of age was in his youth, and the freshness and hopefulness of youth were in his age.

It was under his guidance that I first visited this town, and saw the spots hallowed by the footsteps of the Pilgrims, not darkened by the frown of winter, but touched with the soft lights of departing summer. We were, as Wordsworth says, —

> "A pair of friends, though I was young
> And Matthew seventy-two."

He saw in me the friend and companion of his beloved grandson, William Watson Sturgis, a youth of rare promise, in whose early and sad death so many fond hopes were shattered. How distinctly do the form and presence of the good old man stand before me at this moment! — his venerable head, his benignant countenance, his low voice, which was as incapable of loud or harsh tones as his breast was of harboring the passions that crave such utterance.

In 1820, at the close of the second century of the life of New England, the Pilgrim Society was formed; and it was determined to celebrate the day in a manner which should respond to the strong interest felt in the occasion by all the sons of the Pilgrims. In selecting Mr. Webster as their orator, the Society did but confirm the unanimous choice of public sentiment. He was then in the pride and prime of his magnificent manhood, and had won a national reputation as a lawyer and a statesman. In this presence I need not dwell upon the merits of his admirable discourse; its weight of matter, its strength and simplicity of style, its variety and happy choice of topics, its political wisdom, its dignity of sentiment, and the splendid eloquence of particular passages. Nor need I add how much its substantial claims were aided and enforced by the speaker's remarkable physical gifts, — his noble presence, his vigorous action, and the power of his brow, eye, and voice. In his subsequent life, Mr. Webster often addressed larger bodies, and spoke on more exciting topics, but never did he produce a greater effect than he did upon the select and sympathetic audience which then and there hung upon his lips.

In 1824 the lot fell upon him who was then the choicest flower of New England scholarship, and the other hope — *spes altera* — of New England demonstrative eloquence, Mr. Everett, at that time Professor of Greek Literature in Harvard College. My young friends around me, who saw Mr. Everett in his latter years, when a certain pensive gravity hung over his manner and expression, can hardly imagine what he was in those days, before he had left the primrose path of letters for the steep and thorny way of politics; when the winds of morning were blowing round him, when youth was on the prow and the enchantress Hope at the helm. He was full of radiant life, and overflowing, graceful power. His Plymouth discourse is a beautiful and finished expression of his rare gifts and accomplishments, with striking views and brilliant pictures, the style rich and animated, and the whole glowing with a certain vernal flush of color in harmony with the speaker's youthful aspect and exquisite elocution. To the hearers, it was the unfolding of a web of Tyrian dye, and we who read it will see that the staple is good and the texture firm.

I am not going to compare these two discourses, still less the two men. Either would be an ungracious office. It would be unseemly in New Hampshire and Vermont to dispute which is the more precious gift of Heaven, the granite of the former or the marble of the latter. Let us be thankful for both.

But let me for a moment note a feature of resemblance in the two discourses. Both speakers look at their subject from what may be called a secular and historical point of view. To them the Pilgrims are chiefly interesting as, to use the language of Governor Hutchinson, "the founders of a flourishing town and colony, if not of the whole British colony in North America." I think we can see in both speakers a feeling that the wonderful growth of the country was due, so far as it was due to purely moral causes, not so much to any distinctive traits in the faith and lives of the Pilgrims, making them Separatists from the Church of England and offenders against the law of England, as to the fact that they were Englishmen. Exiles as they were, they brought with them from England the speech and the institutions of the land from whose step-mother frown and malediction they had fled.

A brilliant French writer, whose recent unhappy death our country and his own yet lament, speaking of the progress of an English settlement in Australia, said that if it had been colonized by Frenchmen they would have there only a camp, a café, a theatre, and a prison. Our Fathers brought with them from England two priceless possessions, — the Common Law and King James's Bible: the former a vital organism, not of symmetrical form and graceful outline, but full of the vigorous sap of liberty, and drawing its growth from the soil of the popular heart; the latter, apart from its transcendent claims as a revelation of God to man, in a purely intellectual aspect the most precious treasure that any modern nation enjoys, preserving as it does our noble language at its best point of growth, just between antique ruggedness and modern refinement, embalming immortal truths in words simple, strong, and sweet, that charm the child at the mother's knee, that nerve and calm the soldier in the dread half hour before the shock of battle, that comfort and sustain the soul that is entering upon the valley of the shadow of death! Infinite has been the value of the Bible in training and forming the mind of New England, and through it that of the whole country.

I am one of those who think it unwise to foster ill-will between England and America; and good-will between nations, as between individuals, is maintained by being kind to one another's virtues, and a little blind to one another's faults. Sir Samuel Romilly used to bless the memory of Louis XIV., because his grandfather, by reason of that monarch's revocation of the edict of Nantes, had fled to England, and thus he himself had been born an Englishman and not a Frenchman; and standing on the rock of Plymouth, I confess that I feel somewhat grateful to Archbishop Laud and the Judges of the Star Chamber, because to them we owe it that New England was settled by Englishmen; and thus the progress of our country is traced not by the camp, the café, the theatre, and the prison, but by the meeting-house, the school-house, the court-house, and the ballot-box, all the legitimate fruits of the Bible and the Common Law.

The PRESIDENT. — I take this fitting opportunity, after the allusion by my friend Mr. Hillard to the Orator of 1820, to state that since I took the chair I have received, as a present to the Pilgrim Society, from Francis Russell Stoddard, Esq., the original letter (which I hold in my hand) of Hon. Daniel Webster, accepting the invitation of the Trustees of that Society to deliver his great oration.

It bears date Boston, July 8, 1820, and its text is as follows: —

DEAR SIR, — I am sensible of the respect shown me by the Trustees of the Pilgrim Society, in requesting me to deliver an address before them in December next. I do not hesitate to comply with their wishes, although I cannot but know how many others there are better able than myself to make a performance which should be worthy of the Society and of the occasion.

With great regard, your obedient servant,

DANIEL WEBSTER.

The PRESIDENT. — Mrs. HEMANS's hymn beginning, —

"The breaking waves dashed high," —

will now be sung by SAMUEL B. NOYES, Esq., of Canton.

The hymn was sung with fine effect, Gilmore's band playing an accompaniment; and Mr. Noyes was warmly applauded.

The PRESIDENT. — I will propose as the next sentiment —

The Interests of Learning: Always recognized by our Fathers as a prime necessity of the State.

I will introduce to you Hon. JOHN H. CLIFFORD, President of the Board of Overseers of Harvard College.

SPEECH OF HON. JOHN H. CLIFFORD.

Mr. President, — When I received your very kind note informing me that President Eliot of Harvard College had been compelled by the pressure of his official duties to decline your invitation to these festivities, and requesting, if it were agreeable to me, that I would respond to the sentiment you have just read, I felt that a compliance with your wishes involved a twofold cause of regret, both to the company and to myself.

In any thing having reference to "Harvard College," or to "the interests of learning," I know too well how much we have lost in not having President Eliot himself to answer in their behalf, — one who represents so admirably the latest fruits of that spirit, so honorable to our Fathers, which has blazoned the whole of our history with the evidence of their supreme regard for the great cause of popular education.

He could have told us, without exaggeration, that the ancient University, his recent accession to the government and guardianship of which has given such inspiration to the confidence of its friends, is at least justifying the fond expectations of the Fathers, Pilgrim and Puritan alike, who founded it as one of the chief and favored objects of their highest hopes and aspirations. He could have said, I think with truth, that its present condition and prospects would have satisfied any one of those Pilgrims whom my eloquent friend, the Orator of the Day, in his masterly and unsurpassed portraiture of them, to which we have just listened so delightedly, introduced to us as revisiting the scenes of their earthly pilgrimage, and inquiring what had been the changes and what the advances since they passed to a higher sphere; — and would have prompted him to confess that "the great promise and hope we made and cherished, so far as the College was concerned, has at least been kept and realized."

Why, sir, in their day, to quote the words of one who has been facetiously called the poet "of *all of our Homes*," but whom I regard as eminently entitled, by his immortal tributes to their memory, to be called the Poet of the Pilgrims, —

> "Why, who was in the college, when college first begun?
> Two nephews of the President, and a Professor's son!
> They turned a 'little Injun' by as brown as any bun,
> Lord, how the Seniors knocked about that Freshman class of one!"

A Freshman class of one, Mr. President! while of the ingenuous youth who throng there to-day, — "the rose and expectancy of the fair State," — the members of classes are numbered by hundreds, and the curriculum that is open to them under the guidance of faithful and thoroughly accomplished teachers surpasses in comprehensiveness and completeness more than all the learning of which Brewster, the great scholar of the Pilgrim band, ever dreamed, — more than Christ Church or Baliol, more than all the great Universities of England or the Continent, with their proudest scholarship, could in their day have compassed or comprehended. Does not such a reply as this, which the President of Harvard College could have made to your toast, in language such as would have made my inadequate statement of the contrast seem poor and meagre, furnish us with a satisfactory assurance that the education of their people, which the early Fathers declared must be "the saving hope of the Colony," has been through all our history steadfastly maintained and fostered?

Having thus discharged the vicarious duty you imposed upon me, Mr. President, to the honor of which I had no other title than my official connection with the government of the College, so generously conferred upon me by its sons, — a connection I can never fail at any time or anywhere gratefully to appreciate and acknowledge, — I venture to claim a moment more, to say a word upon a kindred topic, which but for your suggestion and my own sense of loyalty to you and to the occasion, in regarding your request as a command, I had intended to speak.

The early records of the Colony of New Plymouth tell us — and it is a proud evidence of the interest of the Fathers in good learning and popular education — that the proceeds of what was to them a valuable herring fishery at Cape Cod were constituted a fund for the support of a free school in the Colony. This fact, taken in connection with the early establishment of the College, — a period so early that it would not have been strange if the supply of their pressing material wants had engrossed all their thoughts and tasked all their efforts, — "to the end," as they declared, "that good learning may not die out amongst us," has suggested to me a sort of theory, it may be a fanciful one, that there is some subtle and mysterious connection between Education and the Fisheries. And as "the Fisheries" are to-day the great topic of national interest, ay, of more interest than a thousand "Alabamas;" and as we here in Massachusetts mean to support our patriotic President, who has just honored us by sending a telegraphic toast to our table, when he stands up as resolutely as he has done in his recent annual message for the rights of our New England fishermen, — you will pardon me a further illustration or two of the analogy I have suggested between these great interests of the old Colony and Massachusetts Bay. My excellent and eloquent friend, Mr. Hillard, has just told us that he "is one of those who think it unwise to foster ill-will between England and America." I agree with him fully, sir. But at the same time I must declare that I am one of those who deem it eminently wise to require something like equal and exact justice from England; and I venture to say that education will begin to lose its value among us when we shall submit to any restriction upon that great interest of New England, by the fruits of which it has been sustained and cherished. Why, sir, what has the connection between them been throughout our whole Colonial, Provincial, and National history? Let me trace its outline.

Our friend, Professor Agassiz, whom Harvard College, among the great benefits she has conferred upon the country, enticed from his European home to become an American citizen, and bestow upon us the unrivalled fruits of his boundless scientific researches and accomplishments, maintains that there is some pathological or psychological relation between the human brain and the fishes of the sea, — that in the phosphorus of the finny tribes are to be found the peculiar pabulum and nutriment of the brain which make bright, thinking men. Our Fathers, sir, though they may have been ignorant of the Professor's scientific theory, never failed to manifest their high appreciation of the value of these "denizens of the deep." While it is an undisputed fact of history that the only motive which led the Pilgrims of New Plymouth across the ocean was to secure the enjoyment of "freedom to worship God," you know, sir, it has been claimed by some irreverent commentators in reference to the Puritans of Massachusetts, that the chief object of their colonizing adventure was "to fish and trade." The facetious lines attributed to one of the early divines, who, upon a certain occasion familiar to all students of colonial history, made an enforced excursion down Massachusetts Bay, celebrate as among the great providential gifts to the Colony our deep sea fisheries: —

> "That glorious Bay,
> In which — those wonders of the deep —
> The mackerel swim, and porpoise play,
> And crabs and lobsters creep.
> Fish of all kinds inhabit there,
> And swarm the dark abode;
> Here halibut and haddock are,
> And eels, and perch, and cod."

And who of us, whose great privilege it has been to assist at these pious and festive commemorations of the Fathers on this consecrated spot in former years, can forget the saint-like aspect, the serene presence, and the mellifluous voice of another divine of a later age, the worthy successor of John Robinson and Elder

Brewster, the Reverend Dr. Kendall, who always on these occasions, in his fervent thanksgivings to Almighty God, gratefully recognized His good providence, "through which our Pilgrim ancestors were fed, not with the manna of the wilderness, but from the abundance of the sea and the treasures hid in the sand." [13]

Why, Mr. President, what have we done in Massachusetts since the Province Charter united the two Colonies under one jurisdiction, but to hang up as our legislative emblem, in the dome of the Representatives' Hall, that marvellous COD, whose vigilant and unwinking eye keeps watch over our legislators, to see that, when they rise upon its floor, "the tongues and sounds" which reach his ear shall never fail in a patriotic advocacy of the great interests of Education and the Fisheries? It is doubtless to his inspiration and influence that we are indebted for all the voluminous legislation which has been embodied in so many "Acts in addition to the Acts entitled the Acts for the Protection of Alewives in Taunton Great River," — and for the more recent creation of a Commission to restore to their old haunts, in our inland streams and rivers, the trout, the bass, the salmon, and the shad, so ruthlessly driven from them by the improvidence which, in stimulating our manufacturing enterprises, had sacrificed the generous bounty of nature to the insatiate greed of man. To the same source, possibly, we may attribute the honorable distinction of my townsmen of New Bedford, the hardy and adventurous fishermen, who by the banks of Buzzard's Bay "sit on a rock and bob for whale," in having established the first Free Public Library in the Commonwealth, as a municipal institution, supported by the voluntary taxation of the people.

Thus we see how Education and the Fisheries have gone on as mutual supports of each other through all our history: the one, from the earliest humble free school of the Colony to the eldest and most distinguished University of the country; and the other, in the language of old Cowley, "from minnows, to those living islands, whales."

No less conspicuous, Mr. President, if you will permit me to pursue the analogy one step farther, has been the political importance of the Fisheries to all the highest interests of the country. Who that is familiar with our history can forget the stress that was laid upon their maintenance, and their preservation from foreign encroachment, by the great " Colossus of Independence," John Adams, at the close of the war of the Revolution, — or how his illustrious son and successor, John Quincy Adams, as one of the Commissioners at Ghent, enforced their claims to international recognition and observance after the last conflict of arms between the two nations in the War of 1812? And here certainly, on this spot and on this day of commemoration, I should scarcely be justified in not referring to a period earlier than either of these, when a gallant son of our own Plymouth, a lineal descendant of that Governor Winslow whose career has been so fitly and beautifully sketched by the Orator of the Day, led the brave sons of the Colony to the field, among the first of that series of momentous conflicts between the mother country and her ancient foe, for possession of the military posts with which the latter had dotted the continent from the St. Johns to the Mississippi, — conflicts that had their origin in the value which both powers attached to the Fisheries, and which resulted in settling the question whether Protestant England or Catholic France was to be the dominating power in the Colonies of North America.[14] It is not, I think, too much to say, that it was to these colonists of New Plymouth and Massachusetts Bay that Great Britain owed all her power to set up any rights whatever to these Fisheries, in her assertion of which she has treated their descendants, the present hardy fishermen of New England, with so harsh and ungenerous a policy.

Let us hope, Mr. President, that fair and just diplomacy, under the guidance of President Grant, who as a successful and illustrious soldier knows how to value the blessings of Peace, and his able and accomplished Secretary of State, whose name of itself ought to be a guarantee of success in maintaining the rights of our *Fish-ermen*, will soon bring this vexed and vexatious question to a peaceful, honorable, and satisfactory solution. At all events, and in any event, let it be understood at Washington and in Downing Street, as it is in New England, that we are never to surrender, upon any foreign claim or through any foreign interference, any part of this great interest, the first-fruits of which were devoted by our Fathers to the support of free schools and the education of the whole people.

Let me close, sir, with the lines of the same "sweet singer," whom I have already quoted as "the Poet of the Pilgrims." His words are familiar to us all: —

> "God bless those ancient Puritans,
> Their lot was hard enough.
> But honest hearts make iron arms,
> And tender maids are tough.
> So Love and Faith have formed and fed
> Our true-born Yankee stuff,
> And we'll keep the kernel in the shell,
> The British found so rough."

The PRESIDENT. — I wish to say here — both by way of an apology to those gentlemen who have not yet spoken, to which I trust those whom you have already had the pleasure of hearing will close their ears, and a gentle reminder to the audience — that I have had too much to do with political meetings heretofore to put forward all my best speakers in the early part of the evening. We have an abundance of eloquent gentlemen in reserve. I have received by telegraph, from the New England Society of New York, the following : —

The New England Society in the City of New York to the Pilgrim Society at Plymouth, Greeting:

We have redeemed the original purpose of the passengers of the "Mayflower" to land at the mouth of the Hudson, and hope to make up for lost time, and the treachery which led them astray. We have reclaimed a fair portion of this wilderness, and hope in another two hundred and fifty years to win back the whole.

J. H. CHOATE,
President of the New England Society in New York.

The PRESIDENT. — I propose in response,—

The Sons of New England in New York: Whatever they have reclaimed is due to the principles which they have carried with them from the churches and schools and homes of New England; whatever they may hereafter win will be due to the fidelity with which these principles are maintained and perpetuated.

The PRESIDENT. — I will give you as the next toast,—

The Character and Ideas of the Pilgrims: The moulding forces of the Nation.

And introduce to you Rev. JOSEPH P. THOMPSON, D.D., of New York.

SPEECH OF REV. J. P. THOMPSON.

Mr. President, Ladies and Gentlemen, — The encouragement held out in the closing words of Mr. Davis may be accepted as an assurance that some two or three speakers are to come after me, who constitute his reserve. For myself, I count it a happy provision for a speaker when his audience cannot possibly get away. It is no use for you to try to play the Pilgrim just now to the extent of becoming separatists; for if you should get out of *this* "Establishment," where in the world would you go to? You cannot possibly start till the train is ready, and the train will not leave till you have heard those admirable speakers who are to follow me.

What a wonderful day this has been! Rich beyond expression are the treasures that we shall carry away with us. If we came here to be instructed, those of us who thought ourselves most familiar with this story, those of us who have told it over and over again, have yet learned something new from the beautiful setting in which it was presented to us in the church to-day. If we came here for sentiment, how every fountain of feeling within us was unlocked at the first by the rich glory of this wintry sun shining its welcome upon us, and then by the stirring words, the glowing sentiments, the noble thoughts of the Orator! If we came here for the reviving of associations, how every memory has been quickened by the speakers to whom we have listened at this table, and by all the incidents of the day! And yet, enriched as we are, I shall be happy for one, and I think we may all count ourselves happy, if we can carry away with us, as the last total impression of this Jubilee, the impression which was left upon us at the close of the oration, and which is revived in the sentiment just read, that the *character* of the Pilgrims, the character in which their ideas were rooted, from which those ideas sprang, has been the moulding force in this Nation, and must be conserved by us for posterity.

I say it is well to be brought back to this last great thought to carry away with us; for when we are stirred to the depths with sympathetic emotions, it is important that we expend our sympathy at the most effective point, and do not fall into the mistake of the good lady who went to Mount Vernon. The attendant at the place found a lady weeping most bitterly and audibly, with her handkerchief at her eyes. He stepped up to her and said, "Madam, have you lost any thing?" "No, sir," she sobbed. "Are you in any trouble, madam?" "No, sir," she sobbed again. "I saw you weeping." "Ah!" said she, "how can one help weeping at the grave of the Father of his Country?" "Oh, indeed, madam," said he, "that's it! The tomb's over yonder. This is the ice-house." I came here expecting to weep, and certainly expecting to find Plymouth at this time of the year a good deal of an ice-house. I am disappointed in that respect most happily; and now we have been brought so near to the root-idea of the Pilgrim movement that we shall expend our sympathy where it should go, at the point from which we shall receive in return magnetic influences to carry with us to our homes.

That word "magnetic" brings up in my mind an association with which I may in a word enforce the sentiment. The last time I was at Plymouth — a year ago last summer — I was struck more than ever before in my life with the feebleness, the transitoriness, of even the strongest physical impressions in comparison with moral ideas and forces. They were just at that moment bringing into Duxbury the French cable, which happens to-day to be our sole dependence for news from abroad. You all remember the laying of the first Atlantic cable: what enthusiasm was kindled upon two continents; how our country was ablaze with illuminations and bonfires; how the air palpitated with the booming of cannon and the ringing of bells. It was the great event then of the century. The same thing identically was repeated here at Duxbury; yet no man so much as took off his hat in honor of the occasion; — so soon do great physical and material events and interests cease to impress us. It led me to say to myself at that time, "Suppose the grandest miracle in the history of the world, the Resurrection, had been repeated every Sunday, it would soon have ceased to make any more impression than the returning of friends from a journey. It was not the physical resurrection: it was the *life* that was behind it and in it, and the life immortal that it prophesies to all the dying generations of men, that give to the resurrection of Christ its undying power." So it was not the laying of the Atlantic cable, with all the wondrous care of machinery, and all the mighty agencies of steam, and all the nice calculations of mathematics, that could make that event a perpetual wonder or awaken interest in the repetition: the true miracle is the silent throbbing of that invisible force beneath the sea, all untouched by the waves, unbroken by the mountains of the deep that lie over it; and greater than any physical impression made by the forces of nature are the moral impressions made by the force of principle. That power of character which came to Plymouth two hundred and fifty years ago is more potent to-day than the mysterious force of nature, made almost instinct with intelligence, that throbs in sixty seconds through the ocean that the "Mayflower" was sixty days in crossing.

To turn it in another way: suppose the men who came over here at the first had brought with them not ideas, not principles, but the cable and the railway, what manner of nation would this have proved to be? Suppose in those days there had been such facility of transportation that all Erin could have been shipped over upon this colony, what manner of nation would this have been? Nay, it was necessary that first of all this Nation should be grounded in character — *character*, I say. It is not ideas alone. It is barely twenty years since Frenchmen put out the most vaporing ideas of liberty, equality, and fraternity, on paper, in poems, in speeches, everywhere. But what is France to-day? Without a principle, without a flag, without a government, without a cause, without a name, without one rallying cry, such as is wont to appeal to the heart of a great nation, to save her from the crushing destruction that has come upon her. Why? Because of that process of systematic demoralization to which she has been subjected through so many years. France lost her Pilgrim element in the expulsion and massacre of the Huguenots; and her noblest political aspirations have lacked the moral strength that comes of a pure and vigorous religious faith. No strong and stable institutions of freedom can be founded upon a mere declaration of the *rights* of man among his fellows. But the men who came hither brought the fundamental conception of man restored as the child of God. Personality was their root-idea, the personal soul linked to the personal God; and this was greater than King or Parliament, this was greater than Church or Bishop, and no combination against this could ever crush it. And from that root-idea, — not a general notion of man's rights as a citizen, but the religious notion of man's worth as a soul, and of man's worth as a child of God, — sprang the other idea of mutual recognition, each soul to be respected by every other soul; and hence the Compact. And from this came also the idea of kingship and priesthood unto God, pertaining to each personality on board that ship; and hence the free and equal Church. Thus it was that they laid here upon this new shore, upon the borders of this wilderness, the foundation of a nation of moral forces; and when our stern conflict came, it was the revival of those moral forces that saved the Nation. So long as slavery was restricted to a certain section of the country, we might deplore it, our humanity might be touched: it did not reach our consciences. But when the attempt was made to turn every man and woman of us into slave-catchers; when the attempt was made to turn the territory of this Nation into a soil for the extension of slavery, then conscience, the old Pilgrim conscience, the idea of the human soul and its worth, was stirred and roused; and that it was that at length purified and restored and built the Nation. So must it be in whatever conflicts lie before us. The true growth of the Nation is not measured by acres of grain or miles of railway: it must grow by moral ideas and force of character, grow by hugging as its life the principles established here in the Pilgrim character. So great vitality has that character, even when transplanted, that the sons of the Pilgrims may hope, according to the foreshadowings of my respected and honored friend, the President of the New York Society, at last to win back New York itself to justice and virtue.

The PRESIDENT at this period of the dinner stated that it was now a quarter of seven o'clock, and that an express train would leave for Boston at twenty minutes past seven, making no stop; and an accommodation train at half-past seven, stopping at all the way stations.

The PRESIDENT. — The next toast which I propose is —

Religious Toleration: First exemplified in the treatment of Roger Williams by the Pilgrims of Plymouth.

I have the honor of introducing to you Hon. CHARLES S. BRADLEY, of Rhode Island.

SPEECH OF HON. CHARLES S. BRADLEY.

Mr. Chairman, Ladies and Gentlemen, — You kindly, sir, on Monday last, suggested to me that, coming from Rhode Island, I should say a word about Roger Williams on this occasion.

I took some notes from his writings that I might bring you some words from Roger Williams himself; but, at this late hour and in this dim light, I find I cannot read them. Will you allow me, therefore, with but an imperfect recollection of them, to give utterance for a moment to some of those feelings with which upon this theme the heart of every Rhode Islander is full?

Is it not well, sir, as we assemble at the end of this first quarter of a thousand years, to commemorate the Landing of the Pilgrims, whose crowning glory it was that they sought and found upon these Western shores, in the words of the closing line of the hymn we have just heard, —

"Freedom to worship God"? —

Indeed, sir, it is well at this time to remember him, once living here with your forefathers, ever their neighbor and friend, whom your Orator of to-day recognized as "the apostle of soul freedom."

We do not forget the struggles, the controversies, the antagonisms of those early days. We of Rhode Island also remember how our founder, dwelling there apart (for of him, as of his friend Milton, it may be said, —

"Thy soul was like a star, and dwelt apart"), —

how with generous justice he felt and thought and wrote of your forefathers of the Plymouth Colony: "Of the letter from my ancient friend, Mr. Winslow, then Governor of Plymouth, professing his own and others' love and respect to me, yet lovingly advising me (since I was fallen into the edge of their bounds, and they were loath to displease the Bay) to remove but to the other side of the water; and then he said I had the country free before me, and might be as free as themselves, and we should be loving neighbors together; that the then prudent and godly Governor, Mr. Bradford, and others of his godly council, said that I should not be molested nor tossed up and down again while they had breath in their bodies," and "that great and pious soul, Mr. Winslow, melted and visited me at Providence, and put a piece of gold into the hands of my wife for our supply." And even of the Governor of the Massachusetts Bay he writes: "It pleased the Most High to direct my steps into this Bay by the loving private advice of the ever-honored soul, the grandfather, Mr. John Winthrop, who, though he was carried with the stream for my banishment, yet he tenderly loved me to his last breath."

Again Williams writes: "I took his prudent motion as a hint and voice from God; and, waiving all other thoughts and motions, I steered my course from Salem — though in winter snow, which I feel yet — into these parts wherein I may say 'Peniel,' that is, I have seen the face of God."

It was a fine thought of the descendant of that Winthrop, in his oration to-day, that the separate strains and seeming discords of sincere seekers of truth on earth may be blended into perfect harmony in the eternal ear.

Our forefathers were of kingly nature; and amid all that was local and personal, and sharing the infirmities of humanity, they could recognize, respect, and tenderly love each other to their last breath. May not their controversies [Roger Williams termed his works " a musick not fitted to your eares, but to your hearts "] be for us also, at this distant time, blended into harmony by the one great purpose of their lives?

Roger Williams, after long wanderings by sea and land, at last found rest for himself and his companions at the head of Narragansett Bay. He says: " Having, in a sense of God's merciful providence to me in my distress called the place Providence, I desired it might be a shelter for persons distressed for conscience. I then considered the condition of divers of my countrymen." Considering their condition, he divided his property among them. How little could he have foreseen the prosperity of which that gift was the corner-stone! — that " the place Providence " would become, among all the crowding cities of New England, second to but one; that throughout his little colony the inventive brain and cunning hand would make every waterfall, tumbling down the rocks, minister more to the wants of men than the broad, rich prairie of the West. Her growth reminds one of the quaint words of Williams, as applied to another refuge for the distressed: " This confluence of the persecuted, by God's most gracious coming with them, drew boats, drew trade, drew shipping, and that so mightily in so short a time that shipping, trade, wealth, greatness, honor, appeared to fall as out of heaven in a crown or garland upon the head of this poor fisher town."

But it is not in this sequence of his acts that we find Roger Williams's glory. It is that, under his auspices and for the first time in the history of our race, a civil State was founded upon the doctrine of soul liberty. The idea is expressed in the limitation upon the civil compact made by the settlers of Providence in a few simple words, simple and expressive as that description which our Orator to-day cited of the first Sabbath rest of the Pilgrims on yonder island.

The compact which founded the State was binding " *only in civil things*." The limitation at the end of the compact was the impassable barrier which terminated the power of the State. This compact was made by the "masters of families." In the breaking light of new dispensations (by some further Constitutional Amendment, Senator Wilson) are such powers soon to be exercised by those whom, in our day, masters of families themselves obey?

Roger Williams understood the necessity and the limit of civil government. He understood that, in material matters, physical power is the appointed medium of authority; that we must, from our very nature, have in practical life either — to use his own words — "the law of judges and justices of the peace in courts of peace, or the law of arms, the sword and blood." For practical wisdom, law indeed below; but *above*, — for the aspirations of the soul, — *liberty only!*

This thought was not born to mankind in the brain of Roger Williams. The illumination of which my friend, Mr. Hillard, has just spoken with such beauty and truth, did not shine on his face only. Such partiality to one above his fellows does not seem — reverently be it spoken — to be God's method. The light strikes first upon all the mountain peaks. It kindles the vision of poets and philosophers, of sages and Christians. It comes slowly down to us men of affairs, — may I say, Governor Clifford, to governors and judges? — and becomes the common light and property of all men. This doctrine of Roger Williams is found all through history in illuminated minds. Even the heathen poet, speaking of the golden age, says, —

    "Sponte sua, sine lege, fidem rectumque colebat."

The dark and energetic Tertullian says of the Christian faith, —

    "Sponte suscipi debeat, non vi."

Our Orator of to-day has quoted from the lips of a Roman Catholic, the President of the States General of Holland, when the forefathers were there, in an address to that body, the same grand doctrine. It is heard in the sounding march of Milton's prose. — Jeremy Taylor once ascended that mount of vision. It comes from many an humbler voice and pen. In earlier times, it is found in their first confession of faith by the Baptists, to their honor be it said. It was cherished by many of our Pilgrim and Puritan Fathers. Toleration was practised by Friends and Catholics alike on this Western shore. Roger Williams's writings were chiefly devoted to the vindication of the rights of conscience, — to soul liberty. In ponderous volumes, he discusses the "Bloudy Tenent of Persecution for Cause of Conscience" as "contrary to divine and human testimonies;" and, while earnestly seeking after some Church or form wherein his profound convictions of Bible truth might find rest, he grew stronger and clearer in his denial of "the power of the civill sword in spirituals." To this conviction he gave up every thing but life, and that was ever ready for the sacrifice; upon this doctrine he founded his State.

Having established a compact, securing this right, in the wilds of America, Roger Williams crossed the ocean to obtain for it the sanction of the English monarch. Scholar and courtier as he was, a sincere and earnest nature always and everywhere, he obtained "the King's extraordinary favor to this colony as being a banished one, in which His Majesty declared himself that he would experiment whether civil government could consist with such liberty of conscience."

The experiment was a success, — successful in the place of its origin, the State beneath whose greensward he sleeps, and which has clung with unfaltering fidelity to the principle. It was adopted by State after State, —embodied in the Constitution of the United States, which has overarched our prosperity like the protecting heavens. And in our day the great doctrine that civil government shall not be the mere minister of ecclesiastical power finds a home and ascendency even in Rome itself.

In another department in which Roger Williams is entitled to our grateful remembrance, he stood alone. It was, in his own simple phrase, "his soul's desire to do the natives good, and to that end to learn their language." He says, "God was pleased to give me a patient, painful spirit to lodge with them in their filthy, smoky holes, even when I lived at Plymouth and Salem, to gain their tongue." The key to their language he has given us, first compiled in those weary voyages across the Atlantic, when he sought and found a monarch's charter for religious freedom.

Thus living with the Indian and seeking his welfare, they understood each other. He bore in the presence of the Indian, as in that of the monarch, *character*, which, as Dr. Thompson has just truly told us, is the vital force. From it come ideas, institutions, influence. By that character he obtained their confidence; and when he came, a wanderer, to the shores of the Narragansett, he received from their kings, Miantonomi and Canonicus (who distrusted the English), for himself and comrades, what money alone could not have purchased, — a home and a welcome.

That confidence and character did more: they saved the existence of New England. When the Pequots were soliciting the alliance of the Narragansetts with their five or six thousand warriors, for the extermination of the white race, Roger Williams makes his way alone, in an open boat, to the Indian councils, and remained for days and nights among those savages, the only representative of his race.

Rarely in human history do great events so depend upon a single man. By his knowledge of the Indians and their language, and through their confidence in him, he was enabled, under God, to avert the alliance. The whites, with their Indian allies, overcame the Pequots. Forty years of peace ensued, and the infant colonies grew to the stature and vigor of manhood. Had Roger Williams failed in that emergency, the life of our New England would have been nipped in the bud: French colonization would have occupied these shores, with what results the tragedies in Europe to-day disclose. But, sir, we must leave Roger Williams and the forefathers.

We congratulate you that you live here on the eastern coast of our New England, with its clear bright sea and sparkling air, fit nursery for men. To us is given, on its southern coast, that island called by the Indians Aquidneck, the Isle of Peace. Her beautiful shores are now married to civilized life, — the vast and tranquil ocean lingers lovingly around her, — above her the heavens bend in magical and ever-changing hues of beauty, and "the river in the sea," born in the tropics, freighted with their fragrance, brings to those shores with its balmy breath —

"An ampler ether, a diviner air."

We welcome you to our shores. — We accept your welcome here. May we ever unite in commemorating the worth of the past, and receive new inspiration for the present and the future.

The PRESIDENT. — I have a sentiment to which the Hon. GEORGE B. LORING, of Salem, was to have responded; but he is necessarily absent. It is —

The Colony of Cape Ann: The twin sister of the Colony of Plymouth.

I have also a sentiment in honor of the Commonwealth of Massachusetts, to which Governor CLAFLIN was to have responded; but he writes that he is too ill to be present: —

The Nuptials of 1692, *the Union of Massachusetts and the Old Colony:* Their children inhabit every zone; no quarrels have ever alienated them; no divorce can separate them.

Governor CLAFLIN telegraphs me the following toast: —

The Pilgrims did not anticipate the results of the principles they established: may their descendants never in the joy of fruition forsake or forget them.

I have also a sentiment to which Hon. CHARLES FRANCIS ADAMS was to have responded, but he was obliged to leave at an early hour: —

The Mother Country: She maintains the strength of her Government by yielding to the demands of a people inoculated with the principles of our Fathers, so faithfully illustrated by our representatives at her Court.

The PRESIDENT. — I give as the next sentiment, —

The honored Gleaners of all that is wise and instructive in the past: Doubly honored when devoted, through long and active lives, to the great commercial and agricultural interests of the State.

SPEECH OF HON. MARSHALL P. WILDER,

PRESIDENT OF THE NEW ENGLAND HISTORIC-GENEALOGICAL SOCIETY.

Mr. President, and Ladies and Gentlemen, — I thank you, sir, for the kind invitation extended to me to be present on this most interesting occasion. But amidst the beautiful flowers of rhetoric which have bloomed so abundantly around us to-day, and the rich fruits of research of which we have partaken, there is but little for me to offer to this assembly.

You have called on me, sir, to answer for the New England Historic-Genealogical Society, which I have the honor to represent. I am happy to be here, and to respond in her behalf; for it is the object of this Association to treasure up and preserve the history of the forefathers and their descendants, and to transmit it to future generations.

And, sir, I never hear the name of old Plymouth mentioned but I feel the most profound veneration for the Pilgrim Fathers, who here laid the broad foundations of this great Republic, — who here, amidst tears, prayers, and sufferings, planted the germs of a civilization, which has budded, blossomed, and borne fruit in every civilized portion of the globe, — who here established those principles which have sustained our government and made our country what it is; principles which are fast revolutionizing the nations of the Old World, and which, we believe, are destined ultimately to regenerate the kingdoms of this earth.

But the thought which impresses me to-day is the amazing progress in science, art, and in every thing that pertains to the happiness of the human family, since the landing of our Fathers on these shores.

With what anticipation and exultation would our Fathers have looked forward, could they have seen, as we now see, the great future, all to them unknown, of the colony which they were planting? How great the changes that have taken place since that day! Then no village bell chimed for church or school, no temple for worship, save the "sounding aisles of the dim woods," canopied by the blue ether above: now our cities, towns, and villages rise as by magic, and adorn our hill-sides and broad valleys; and now our churches, schools, and benevolent institutions, like manna from the skies, are scattered broadcast throughout the length and breadth of our happy land.

Then the "Mayflower" crept timidly along this shore, waiting for wind and tide; now our gigantic steamers dash up our mighty rivers, and across lakes and oceans, despite of wind or tide or storm.

Then the voice of our Fathers echoed in the dark forest only to return and die upon the shore; now the voice of their descendants is heard in every language and land, and to-day, through the genius of their sons, it speaks, with lightning flash, throughout the earth.

Then the track of the wild beast and the trail of the wild man had only furrowed the surface of our continent: now a net-work of intercommunication, with arteries scarcely less numerous than those of the human system, encompasses and covers our broad domain; and through it flow the trade, commerce, and intercourse, not only of our own people, but it furnishes also a great highway across the continent for the people of all other nations and all time.

With what surprise would that little Pilgrim band have looked forward, could they have anticipated that, in two and a half centuries, their population of a hundred souls, together with the little colony in Virginia, and a handful of Dutch on the shores of the Hudson, would be multiplied into forty millions! or, still more wonderful, could they have passed with us to-day by the same old Rock, while celebrating the fifth jubilee of their landing, and look forward, as we now look, to the sixth jubilee, when, according to the last estimates, that population will be increased to one hundred millions of souls. Would they not say, " Truly this work is marvellous in our eyes: a little one has become a thousand, and a small one a great nation"?

And how would they have rejoiced, when partaking of their scanty meal of five kernels of corn, or when rendering special thanks for the annual crop of twenty bushels of corn and six bushels of oats and peas, — how would their voices have broken forth in hallelujahs of thanksgiving to the God of harvest, could they have had a vision of the thousand millions of bushels in our annual crop, — a crop of grain sufficient to give a bushel each to every man, woman, and child on the face of the globe!

How would the soul of the generous Peregrine White have swelled with joy, had he known, when planting his apple-tree at Marshfield, that this fruit would become an article of daily food, or that his orchard of one tree would be magnified into orchards of twenty thousand or more trees of a single variety! And although it is recorded that Governor Winthrop some years after had a good store of pippins, yet neither of these gentlemen could have foreseen the influence of their example in New England, not to speak of three counties in New York that produce annually five hundred thousand barrels of apples, or the annual crop of our country, sufficient to regale the appetites of every human being in the United States. Think what Governor Endicott would have said, if he had been told that the planting of his first pear-tree at Salem would be multiplied into thousands of orchards, some of which in our own State contain eight hundred or one thousand varieties, all better than his own; and that, instead of being trained and nursed in the gardens of the opulent, this fruit should be enjoyed by the western pioneer on the Pacific coast as well as by the eastern magistrate, from whence we have received, within a few days, pears weighing four pounds and nine ounces.

But I must not prolong this train of thought. The more I contemplate the history of this country, the more I reflect on the great moral and political events which have elevated our nation to heaven in point of privilege, the more I am impressed with the obligation to do something for its advancement, something to aid this grand march of improvement. And how sublime the record of the past! The discovery of this continent, how momentous in its results! The development of its resources, how wonderful and grand! The example of its people, how great and good!

No event since the birth of our blessed Saviour has been fraught with such mighty issues as the mission of our Fathers to this land. And how would their souls have been moved with joy and thanksgiving, could they, when kindling the glimmering fires of civil and religious freedom, have had but a glimpse of the bow of promise which irradiates the present day! Already the day-star of glory has arisen; and, like that which led the wise men of the East, culminating over Judea's plains, the star of empire, leading the nations of the earth, finds its meridian height over this western world. How marvellous the story! It is only one-fourth of a thousand years since the eagle of liberty first rested her foot on our rock-bound coast, — only two hundred and fifty years! And now to-day she stands perched on yonder mountain peak, stretching her broad wings from sea to sea, and proclaiming to the uttermost ends of the earth, LIBERTY OF CONSCIENCE! FREEDOM FOR ALL! SERVITUDE FOR NONE!

The next toast will be —

The Old Town of Boston: Though Plymouth had ten years the start, she is not annoyed at being distanced in the race; for she knows the jockey who wins is an Old Colony Boy.

I have the pleasure of introducing to you Hon. N. B. SHURTLEFF, Mayor of Boston, whom we claim as a son of the Old Colony.

RESPONSE OF HON. N. B. SHURTLEFF.

Mr. President, Ladies and Gentlemen, — For remembering so kindly the city of Boston on this pleasant occasion, my fellow-citizens, who are so largely represented here to-day, will be very grateful to the good people of this ancient town, — descendants of renowned worthies, the forefathers of the good old Colony of New Plymouth. I am well pleased also that you recognize me as one closely allied to the Old Colony people; for, although a native of Boston, I feel proud that every one of my American ancestors were born within the jurisdiction of the Plymouth Colony, and that every drop of blood that flows through my veins comes directly from the Pilgrims.

On this, the shortest day of the year, I have come, as a humble Pilgrim, to the hallowed homes of my revered ancestors to spend with you the longest night our season affords, in order to recall the mighty deeds which they of old performed, and to renew with you my fealty to those principles that led them in such an inclement season of the year to brave the dangers of an almost unknown ocean, to establish a new home on inhospitable shores, and a colony determined on self-government, — that surest guarantee of civil and religious liberty; and for the enactment of laws, which they themselves would make, enforce, and willingly obey; and for the enjoyment of perfect freedom in religious worship, untrammelled by rules, observances and usages inflicted by the persecutions of uncompromising hierarchies. Here, on this spot, made sacred by the sufferings, hardships, and endurances of the self-exiled Pilgrims, we have gathered together to commemorate the great event that occurred just two hundred and fifty years ago, and to pay our tribute of gratitude to those most estimable persons; and, in viewing the places where they once dwelt, toiled, and worshipped, and in recalling to mind their virtues and good principles, to show our appreciation of their lives, character, and actions, and a proper regard for their memories. We have come to this particular place, that we may be able to rejoice at the excellence of these our Fathers in the very field of their early privations and labors, and to reciprocate congratulations that the grand object which they attained by coming to New England has been so faithfully preserved for our enjoyment. Let us be careful to preserve the good inheritance which our Fathers have left us, and let us transmit it unimpaired to the latest posterity, that coming generations may hail this natal day, as we do now, as that on which was born the freest of all the governments of the world. Forget not the pledges of that little compact of forty-one men, written perhaps in twenty lines and signed in Provincetown Harbor, — the first written constitution the world ever knew. More potent has been that simple instrument of only two hundred words than have been all the charters displayed on parchment, with emblazonry, and sanctioned by the broadest and greatest seals of princely potentates.

When one comes to Plymouth, Mr. President, the first inquiry is for the landmarks of the olden time and the vestiges of the first-comers. Some of these have been shown us to-day, as we have passed over the roads and through the by-ways, once the accustomed walks of your venerated predecessors. We have paid our wonted passing respects to the solitary old Rock that so opportunely served in 1620 as a landing place for the Pilgrim voyagers, and as a monument for all future time of one of the most memorable events in the history of our country. More enduring will be the fame, and the presence too, of that rough unsculptured boulder, than chiselled statue or lofty memorial of smoothly hammered ashler. As we marched by the water-side and beneath the sacred hillock that overlooks the placid waters of the harbor that so kindly bore upon its bosom the Pilgrim vessels, we have instinctively bowed our heads in filial veneration of the little band of adventurers who came to this spot two hundred and fifty years ago, and one-half of whom were gathered to their earthly rest beneath its sod during that dreadful first winter of the colonists of New Plymouth [15]; and as we trod our way through your Leyden Street, with its ancient dwellings, genial reminders of the pleasant days of the past, we could almost call back to their first " meersteads and garden plots " our well-beloved forefathers, and behold each with his family standing in his appointed lot.

I had hoped, Mr. President, that you would have had sufficient time to have taken us around and shown more of your interesting memorials of the olden time. What recollections and associations of the past would have been thus awakened! Your old town brook, that afforded in days of yore a safe dockage for the Pilgrims' pinnace, and an abundance of the famous good Old Colony staple that we are told could once run up to Billington Sea as easily as now down Taunton River; the Pilgrim spring that supplied the temperate beverage of the first comers; the hill at our south where first appeared aboriginal friendship, — these are marks of interest which we could have revisited with advantage as well as with antiquarian pleasure. From yonder sacred hill, where so peacefully repose the once active spirits of your town, you could have pointed out innumerable objects of interest. Upon the brow of that eminence are gathered the mortal remains of worthies whose names are most indelibly fixed in our memories, and the remembrance of whom is always dearest in our thoughts. On this day, sir, our minds should be entirely given to the past; and we all hope to be pardoned if we indulge somewhat personally in the glorious recollections of the virtues of our predecessors. Recreant, indeed, sir, should we all be, were we to forget on this occasion the great results that have emanated from the good principles, the noble daring, the patient sufferings, and the estimable attributes of our ancestry.

I have come here to-day, my friends, to rejoice with you that the "May Flower," the "Fortune," and the "Ann" found their haven of rest on these shores; and however much we of Boston may admire and reverence the Puritan Fathers of the old Massachusetts Colony who founded our ancient metropolis, we are always willing, and at all times ready, to yield the palm to the Plymouth Pilgrims, who, placing liberty of conscience high above all other things, first planted their hopes upon the soil where we are now congregated to do them just reverence.

The PRESIDENT. — I propose as the last sentiment,—

The Sons of New England beyond our Borders: Under whatever flag they live, they illustrate and reflect with honor and pride Pilgrim ideas and Pilgrim principles.

This sentiment was responded to by Hon. T. STERRY HUNT, President of the New England Society in Montreal.

SPEECH OF HON. MR. HUNT.

It is with great pleasure that I to-day visit for the first time a spot which from my childhood I have been taught to look upon as the birthplace not only of a nation, but of a new political and social order. With no less pleasure do I appear here among you at this banquet as the representative of the New England Society of Montreal. It might not seem necessary that I should bring with me any other credentials than those given me by my title of President of the Society, were it not that our Society has so enlarged its scope as to include Americans, not of New England birth, who may be residents in Canada, and did I not wish to-day to glory in my New England birth and lineage, surely a pardonable pride on an occasion like the present. Under the old *régime* in France, certain honors of the Court were accorded only to those who could prove a long descent from gentle blood, unmingled with any base plebeian stain, and who by heraldic laws were entitled to quarter the armorial bearings of so many Frankish barons or conquering crusaders. If in this land of ours, where all are sovereigns, we are to recognize any hereditary title of rank or distinction, it should be for such as can claim a descent from those brave Englishmen, who, through their faith in God and in the rights of man, conquered the wilderness, subdued savages, and built up on these shores our free institutions. For myself, a native of Connecticut, I can boast that for more than two hundred years my ancestors, on both sides, have been dwellers on New England soil, and, though not of the little band of the "Mayflower," may claim a place among the forefathers of this Commonwealth and of Rhode Island. Although the pursuit of science has led me to spend some years of my life in Canada, " my heart, untravelled, fondly turns" to my home and that of my fathers; and I come here to-day, a reverent pilgrim, feeling that earth has for me but one more hallowed spot than this.

The sentiment which we have just heard from the chair recognizes the fact that the influences which have gone out from this centre have passed beyond the borders of our great Republic. It is significant that New England Societies exist in Montreal and Toronto; but we must look farther and wider, if we would measure the extent of those influences in the British American Provinces, and in doing so must glance at a chapter in our history which is often lost sight of.

Emerson has beautifully compared old England to the banyan-tree of the East, whose branches, touching the earth, take root and grow to be trees themselves. Grandest of all these offshoots was the branch which, stretching far over the ocean, two hundred and fifty years since, took root in this seemingly sterile soil, and has since grown to be a mighty tree whose branches, in their turn, have planted themselves throughout our land, until they overshadow a continent. To-day, on the shores of the great lakes, in the valley of the Mississippi, and
"Where the sun, with softer fires,
Looks on the vast Pacific's sleep,"

beside the golden gate of the West, "the children of the Pilgrim sires" keep with us high festival beneath the shadow of that tree whose leaves are for the healing of the nation.

But of the tree which struck root on Plymouth Rock, there is an offshoot beyond our border, about which I would say a few words to-day. There went out from New England, three generations ago, a colony of men, and of women too, who have since played in the history of this continent a part honorable alike to the land of their birth and the place of their voluntary exile. I speak of the expatriated Tories of the Revolution, or, as they loved to call themselves, the United Empire Loyalists. To-day, when the actors in the great drama of the War of our Independence have passed away, and the strifes and hatreds of that time are forgotten, a descendant of those who fought and conquered them may be permitted to speak a word in behalf of the old New England Loyalists and their children. Let me here say that a residence of many years in Canada has no whit diminished my love and reverence for the founders of the American Republic, whose names, whose cause, and whose honor I hold no less sacred than that of our Pilgrim forefathers. The logic of events has doubtless already taught many of the sons of the old Loyalists to regret the mistaken zeal and the errors of their ancestors; yet it is not without pride that they look back to the sufferings and sacrifices of that band of adherents to the crown, who became exiles for conscience' sake. They were erring sons who went out from their father's house, but have after all proved themselves no unworthy scions of the old stock. That they carried with them much of the spirit of their ancestors, the subsequent history of these self-exiled New Englanders has abundantly shown. It is not too much to say that what is most worthy of honor in the history of the English-speaking population of the British American Provinces is to be traced to the American Loyalists and their descendants, who left this country at the time of our War of Independence.

It is not an easy task for us to-day to put ourselves in the position of those men, after the experience of nearly a century has justified the wisdom of our ancestors in resisting even to blood the authority of the Crown, that they might win for themselves and for their children a free press, free commerce, and the right of self-government. The patriots of the Revolution at first claimed no more than these, and demanded less of Great Britain than she has since accorded to those North American Colonies which still own her sway. We find, however, among the two thousand souls who at the time of the Revolution left the shores of Massachusetts, adherents to the Crown, a list of names which any cause might be proud to claim. They were, very many of them, of the best blood of New England, — men of every profession, jurists and divines as well as merchants and yeomen. No small proportion of the graduates of Harvard and Yale were among those who then sought a home on the banks of the St. Lawrence, or on the inhospitable shores of the Acadian provinces. These men were not altogether recreant to the spirit of their sires, though their love to the Crown, and to the English Church, to which very many of them adhered, led them to cling to the British cause. They showed the ancient spirit by surrendering wealth, position, and friends, and betaking themselves to a new land as their fathers had done before them.

I may be permitted by a few examples to show the part which the Loyalists and their descendants have played in the country of their adoption, where their names have always stood foremost in law, in letters, and in statesmanship. I may name Jonathan Sewall, of Boston, the friend of John Adams, whose son was for many years Chief Justice of Lower Canada; the late Sir Brenton Haliburton, jurist, historian, and humorist, a native of Rhode Island; Sir John Wentworth, Governor of New Hampshire, and afterwards of Nova Scotia, whose descendants in Canada still inherit the great qualities of their race; Upham, of Brookfield, a name and a family in honor both in Nova Scotia and in Massachusetts; Coffin, of Boston, whose descendants are prominent both in New Brunswick and in Canada; Rowth, of Salem, late Chief Justice of Newfoundland; Jarvis, of Connecticut, who held a similar office; Winslow, of Plymouth, the orator of the day at our festival here one hundred years ago, afterwards judge and administrator of the government of New Brunswick.[16] Putnam, Wetmore, Botsford, and Bliss, are names not less famous in the history of this colony; and the grandson of the latter, the second judge of his name, descended from the Wilmots, a Loyalist family of Long Island, is now Governor of New Brunswick. Howe, President of the Federal Council, is the son of a Bostonian. Aylwin and Day, now ornaments of the Quebec Bar, are of the same good stock.

If from the example of our Montreal New England Society I might enlarge my limits, so as to take in names from others of the old thirteen colonies, I could add the Robinsons, of Toronto, represented by the late Chief Justice Sir John Beverley Robinson; the Stuarts, of Quebec, descendants of the late Sir James Stuart; the Ogdens and the Smiths, of New York; Sir William Logan, son of a New York Loyalist; Egerton Ryerson, the founder of the common school system of Upper Canada, whose father was from New Jersey; and many others, whose names and titles to distinction would occupy us too long. The record is already sufficient to show that the New Englanders of to-day have no cause to be ashamed of the sons of the United Empire Loyalists.

But I must not forget that it is not as their representative that I appear before you on this occasion. Adventurous sons of New England have in the present generation contributed their full share to develope in various directions the resources of the British American Provinces. In bringing forth the wealth of the forests and the mines, and in every branch of manufacture, New England skill and industry have been prominent, until the name of " Yankee " has there become synonymous with enterprise, thrift, and success. The Government of the Dominion places no barrier to their political advancement; and native Americans of Whig descent are to-day to be found in the House of Commons and in the Senate, side by side with the children of the old New England Tories. An American of New England name and lineage, Howland of New York, a successful merchant and a minister of finance, is now Governor of the Province of Ontario.

And now to repeat a question often asked me, What is the destiny of these British American Colonies? The old imperial idea, which made the greatness of Rome, which is the strength of resuscitated Germany, and makes us to-day a great and strong Nation, is apparently losing its hold on the governing class in England. The policy of abandoning her foreign possessions now finds advocates among the statesmen of Great Britain; and the dismantled fortresses of her North American Provinces, from which the last gun and the last soldier are being removed, tell us plainly that, for good or for evil, Britain is leaving the colonies to themselves. Meanwhile the vision of a great united empire rises before the eyes of Canadian statesmen, who dream of a new nation stretching to the northward of us from sea to sea. Such a conception shows a great progress in national life, and is fitted to call forth the best energies of the Canadian people. Of one thing we may be certain: that this great country, with its immense resources, has before it a noble future; and that, whether as a new nationality or as a part of this great Republic, American ideas and New England virtues will always be found powerful influences in guiding and in shaping its destinies.

The PRESIDENT. — It is now quarter past seven o'clock: the trains are ready; and as I welcomed the coming, I now speed our parting, guests.

THE BALL.

THE programme of the Committee of Arrangements closed with a grand ball in the evening, in Davis Hall, which was attended by about four hundred ladies and gentlemen, and exceeded in brilliancy any thing of the kind ever before undertaken in Plymouth. The hall was brilliantly lighted, and decorated with good taste and judgment. The floor was covered with white canvas, and the entries and stairs were carpeted to the outer door. In front of the gallery over the stage the date 1620, and at the opposite end of the hall the date 1870, were exhibited in jets of gas, adding much to the brilliancy of the scene. The names of CARVER, BRADFORD, WINSLOW, STANDISH, WHITE, ALDEN, BREWSTER, and CHILTON, were displayed in green on each side of the two dates; and portraits of EDWARD WINSLOW, JOSIAH WINSLOW, PENELOPE WINSLOW, the wife of Josiah, JOHN WINSLOW, GEORGE WASHINGTON, EPHRAIM SPOONER, JOHN DAVIS, JAMES THACHER, JOHN TRUMBULL, JOHN ALDEN, and JAMES KENDALL, hung on the walls. Baskets of rich flowers were suspended from the columns, bearing in their fragrance constant testimony to the delicate taste with which the details of the programme were carried out.

A coffee-room was open from the beginning to the close of the ball; and the supper-room, which was opened at twelve o'clock, was abundantly supplied until the last dance was finished.

The music, furnished by Gilmore's Band, consisted of nine pieces, under the direction of Mr. JOHN T. BALDWIN as prompter; and, under the careful management of the floor managers, the ball was conducted to a brilliant conclusion at about four o'clock in the morning.

With the last strains of the music in Davis Hall, the Celebration closed; and while those upon whom its labors and responsibilities rested congratulate themselves upon its successful consummation, all who participated in its ceremonies and festivities will remember with ever-increasing pleasure the Two Hundred and Fiftieth Anniversary of the Landing of the Pilgrims.

APPENDIX.

LETTERS IN REPLY TO INVITATIONS.

Hon. WM. T. DAVIS, Plymouth, Mass.

DEAR SIR, — I am in receipt of your letter of the 12th inst. inviting me to attend the Celebration of the Anniversary of the Landing of the Pilgrims. It would afford me great pleasure to be present upon an occasion of so much interest; but it will be impossible to leave the capital at that time, and I am compelled to decline your very cordial invitation.

Respectfully yours,

U. S. GRANT.

EXECUTIVE MANSION, Nov. 19th, 1870.

WASHINGTON, Dec. 1, 1870.

MY DEAR SIR, — Gratifying as it would be to participate in your Celebration, I regret to have to reply that public duties here prevent the acceptance of the invitation with which I have been honored.

Very truly yours,

SCHUYLER COLFAX.

Hon. W. T. DAVIS.

DEPARTMENT OF STATE,
WASHINGTON, Dec. 14, 1870.

Messrs. WM. T. DAVIS, WM. H. WHITMAN, &c., Plymouth, Mass., Committee of Arrangements.

GENTLEMEN, — Your invitation to be present at the Celebration of the Two Hundred and Fiftieth Anniversary of the Landing of the Pilgrims at Plymouth presents a temptation to which I would be glad to yield, but for the pressure of official duties which will require my presence here.

Accept, I beg you, my thanks for the invitation.

I have the honor to be,
Very respectfully yours,
HAMILTON FISH.

TREASURY DEPARTMENT,
Office of the Secretary, Nov. 16, 1870.

DEAR SIR, — I regret to learn from your letter of the 12th inst. that I accidentally neglected to reply to your former letter extending to me an invitation to be present at the Two Hundred and Fiftieth Anniversary of the Landing of the Pilgrims at Plymouth.

I presented to the President your invitation to him, and I also said a word in favor of his accepting it; but I inferred from his conversation, what I had reason to expect from my knowledge of affairs, that he would feel compelled to decline. I fear, also, that it will not be in my power to be present, although I should esteem it a great privilege to unite with the descendants of the Pilgrims in celebrating their virtues and heroism.

The invitations enclosed with your letter of the 12th inst. will be presented to the gentlemen for whom they are designed.

I have the honor to be,
Very respectfully, your obed't serv't,
GEO. S. BOUTWELL.

Hon. WILLIAM T. DAVIS,
Chairman of Committee of Arrangements.

DEPARTMENT OF THE INTERIOR,
WASHINGTON, Nov. 23, 1870.

WM. T. DAVIS, WM. H. WHITMAN, and others,
Committee of Arrangements for Pilgrim Society.

GENTLEMEN, — Your invitation to be present at the Celebration of the Landing of the Pilgrims at Plymouth, on the 21st of December, is received.

I regret to say that pressure of official business will compel me to decline your very cordial invitation. You have my best wishes for the success of the Celebration.

Yours respectfully,
C. DELANO.

POST OFFICE DEPARTMENT,
WASHINGTON, D. C., Nov. 17th, 1870.

WILLIAM T. DAVIS, Esq.

DEAR SIR, — I have the honor to acknowledge the receipt of your invitation to attend the Celebration of the Two Hundred and Fiftieth Anniversary of the Landing of the Pilgrims at Plymouth, and to return you my thanks. It is a source of much regret that official duties will oblige me to deny myself the pleasure of being present on that interesting occasion.

Very respectfully yours,

J. A. J. CRESWELL.

DEPARTMENT OF JUSTICE,
WASHINGTON, Dec. 6th, 1870.

WILLIAM T. DAVIS, Esq., and others, Committee of Arrangements of the Pilgrim Society, Plymouth, Mass.

GENTLEMEN, — I have received, through Governor Boutwell, an invitation to your Celebration of the Two Hundred and Fiftieth Anniversary of the Landing of the Pilgrims at Plymouth, on Wednesday the 21st.

It would give me great pleasure to participate in the celebration of so interesting an anniversary, — interesting both on account of the character of the men who landed at Plymouth in 1620, and of the important influence of that character in forming the literature, the politics, and the morals of the continent. But the necessity of being in Georgia at that time, if permitted by my duties to be absent from the capital, will deny me the pleasure of accepting your invitation.

Very respectfully yours,

AMOS T. AKERMAN.

WAR DEPARTMENT,
WASHINGTON, Nov. 17, 1870.

SIR, — Please express to the members of your Committee my thanks for their invitation to the Celebration of the Pilgrim Society on the 21st December, and my regret that other engagements will interfere with its acceptance.

Very respectfully,

Your obedient servant,

WM. W. BELKNAP,
Secretary of War.

Hon. WM. T. DAVIS.

UNITED STATES SENATE CHAMBER,
WASHINGTON, Dec. 12th, 1870.

Hon. WILLIAM T. DAVIS.

MY DEAR SIR, — It is with great regret that I have to reply to your kind invitation to attend the Two Hundred and Fiftieth Anniversary of the Landing of the Pilgrims, by saying that the pressure of engagements here will not permit me to be present. My reply would have been made at an earlier date, had not my anxiety to be with you on that occasion led me to delay, in the hope that I would be able to participate in your meeting, and pay, in person, my tribute to the venerable men and women who laid the foundation of the glory of New England.

Wherever the law is respected, justice administered, civilization advancing, there are the sons of New England; and as, with the westward course of empire, they climb the mountains and traverse the plains, they cast ever a longing look of tender remembrance towards the ancient seat. And it would have been especially agreeable to me, had it been possible, to be with you, and assure you of the respect which New England men in the West cherish for their birthplace; how proudly they claim a share of its renown, and how anxiously they watch the course of its scholars and statesmen in the progress of public affairs, for their inspiration and guidance.

Very respectfully and truly yours,

MATT. H. CARPENTER.

WASHINGTON, D. C., Dec. 19th, 1870.

GENTLEMEN, — I had, until Saturday, expected to attend the memorial services to be held at Plymouth, on the 21st inst., to which you have honored me with an invitation; but I now find I shall be held here by unavoidable public duties.

I regret this exceedingly, as I had anticipated a gathering of gentlemen worthy of the men whose advent to these shores they propose to celebrate, and whom it would be a pleasure to me to meet.

But I am sure the whole body of Pilgrims would rise up against me, should I neglect a service due to the living, to pay a tribute of homage and gratitude to the dead. The distinguishing peculiarity of the Pilgrims was their unswerving loyalty to duty. In this was their pre-eminence over other emigrants of their or preceding ages. It was this which gave permanence and final success to the Colony.

If they had been more skilled in state craft, and less in the creed of a faith which recognized the individual responsibility of man, the simple polity of their church would never have become the basis of the pure democracy of our town governments, which by combination developed into the representative governments of the State and the Nation. The creed which held each responsible to God for his acts made liberty in the State as essential as in the Church, and demanded universal education as a right springing from man's responsibility.

But the highest fruit of their faith was character. Constant meditation upon divine truths imparted an elevation to their lives which prepared them to meet and surmount the perils and hardships they encountered, and to hand down those transcendent qualities which have sustained and inspired their descendants through all the events of our unparalleled history. The sentiments of the Pilgrims have left an imperishable impress upon our national institutions and character.

God grant that they may not cease to be held in grateful remembrance by their children till their virtues shall cease to ennoble our national life.

With thanks for your kind remembrance, and regrets that I cannot be with you,

I am, with great respect,
Your obedient servant,
J. W. PATTERSON.

HORNELLSVILLE, N. Y., 28th Nov. 1870.

MY DEAR SIR, — Your two favors have followed me to this place, where I am for a day. It is with great regret that I abandon the opportunity with which you honor me. But my engagements at Washington make it impossible for me to be with you on the Pilgrim Anniversary. The Senate will then be in session, and I never allow myself to leave my seat under any temptation. In this fidelity I try to imitate the Pilgrims.

Faithfully yours,
CHARLES SUMNER.

Hon. WM. T. DAVIS.

WASHINGTON, Nov. 22, 1870.

DEAR SIR, — I did my best to secure for you the attendance of the President. You will learn from his answer, when it comes, that it has been done in vain.

I should be glad to go myself, if it were possible to get away from Washington at that time, of which there is no hope.

Truly yours,

J. C. B. DAVIS.

Hon. WM. T. DAVIS.

HEADQUARTERS ARMY OF THE UNITED STATES,
WASHINGTON, D. C., Nov. 19, 1870.

W. T. DAVIS, Esq., Plymouth, Mass.

DEAR SIR, — I have your very friendly letter of November 15, and assure you of my sense of the extreme honor you design for me, in connection with the proposed Celebration of the Two Hundred and Fiftieth Anniversary of the Landing of the Pilgrims on "Plymouth Rock." I don't see how I can possibly come; for I must go to an army meeting, at Cleveland, Ohio, next week, and have also particularly promised to attend the New England dinner at Delmonico's, New York, on the 22d of December next. I have not yet seen the President, and don't know what answer has been sent; but it seems to me he can hardly spare the time at that season of the year. Should he, however, agree to go to Plymouth, and should he request me to go along, I would construe it in the nature of an obligation that would release me from the prior promise to be with the New England Society of New York. Though not a native of New England, I always remember that both my parents were born at Norwalk, Connecticut, and shall ever cherish their memory and virtues. This may entitle me to full fellowship with the New England Societies, though from association I usually claim affiliation with the Broad Field of the Great West, with which my associations have been more intimate and more closely identified. If in life, however, I can blend all parts of our Union into the hearty fellowship which a common nationality, common history, and a common destiny have decreed, I surely will attempt it.

Every thing you have written begets a desire to be present, and witness so interesting an occasion; but I fear the chances are against me. I am none the less obliged to you for the cordial manner in which you have invited me to accept the hospitalities of Plymouth during the commemoration of the Two Hundred and Fiftieth Anniversary of the Landing of the Pilgrims.

With great respect, &c.,
W. T. SHERMAN, *Genl.*

WASHINGTON, D. C., Dec. 6, 1870.

WM. T. DAVIS, Esq.

DEAR SIR, — I certainly admire your perseverance, and only regret that for the display of this virtue you have so indifferent a subject. You surely have been most kind, and are entitled to my heartiest thanks; but still I remain of the opinion that it would be improper for me to attempt so much. Let me repeat. I must attend here, during the night of Monday the 19th, a ball given for the benefit of the poor, of which Mrs. Sherman is a patroness, and I am announced as a manager. I must leave early next morning, the 20th, for Philadelphia, to attend the grand opening, that evening, of Rothermell's picture of Gettysburg, in compliment to, and by earnest invitation of, General Meade. If I am to accept your invitation, I would have to hurry away, in order to reach Plymouth by noon of the 21st; then, at 5, P.M., hurry away to get to Boston in time for the train for New York, where, on the 22d, I would have to dine out, and go straight to the New England dinner, at Delmonico's, at 9, P.M. Now I leave it to you, if flesh and blood, weakened by fifty years' hard work, ought to be taxed in that style; and would I not be likely to reach the feast of the wits of New York a dull guest?

I must again ask your kind indulgence to spare me such a race after pleasure; for I know you respect me too highly to wish me to attempt what would be hard work, instead of a personal gratification to myself or to my friends.

I hope I may live for another occasion, when it would be a real treat to stand among the descendants of the Pilgrim Fathers, upon the very spot which they hallowed by their steps.

With great respect,
Your friend,
W. T. SHERMAN, *General.*

LOWELL, Nov. 18, 1870.

MY DEAR MR. DAVIS, — Pity me! I am obliged to attend a meeting of the Board of Managers of the National Asylum, on the 19th, at Washington, which will last for three days, so that I cannot help to commemorate the Pilgrims; but I will do all I can to induce the President to go, although, it being just before the holidays, I have not much hope of my efforts.

Yours truly,

BENJ. F. BUTLER.

Mr. WM. T. DAVIS, Plymouth, Mass.

WASHINGTON, Dec. 10, 1870.

SIR, — I have the honor to acknowledge the receipt of an invitation to attend the Pilgrim Society's Celebration of the Two Hundred and Fiftieth Anniversary of the Landing of the Pilgrims at Plymouth, Dec. 21, 1870. It is scarcely probable that I shall be able to leave Washington at that time; but should it be in my power to do so, I shall esteem it a great pleasure to participate in the celebration of the great event which it is proposed thus to honor.

Very respectfully,

Your obedient servant,

N. P. BANKS.

Hon. WM. T. DAVIS.

WASHINGTON, D. C., Dec. 1, 1870.

MY DEAR SIR, — I have earnestly hoped that I should be able to accept your invitation to attend the meeting of the Pilgrim Society of Plymouth, on the 21st of December; but I find that it will not be possible for me to do so.

The thought of meeting that Society, to aid in celebrating the Two Hundred and Fiftieth Anniversary of the Landing of the Pilgrims, was so agreeable to me, that it has been with difficulty that I am compelled to abandon it.

Please present my regrets to the Society, and accept for them and for yourself my thanks for their kind invitation.

Very truly yours,

J. A. GARFIELD.

Hon. WM. T. DAVIS.

BRITISH LEGATION,
WASHINGTON, Nov. 18, 1870.

Hon. WM. T. DAVIS, Ch.

Sir Edward Thornton presents his compliments to the Committee of Arrangements of the Pilgrim Society, and begs to express his regret that he fears it will be out of his power to avail himself of their kind invitation for the 21st of December next; for it is at a time of the year when his official duties render it very difficult for him to absent himself from Washington.

STATE OF MAINE EXECUTIVE DEPARTMENT,
AUGUSTA, Dec. 17, 1870.

MY DEAR SIR, — On receiving your letters, which had followed my track for some time, I wrote you a hurried letter last evening, saying that I thought it doubtful if I could manage to be with you at Plymouth. Looking at the business which now opens, and the imperative engagements which unfold to claim every moment of the closing year, I still find it doubtful, if not impossible. I have unavoidable engagements of a public nature on the day before and day after the 21st, and it would drive me fast and far to attempt to reach you and get back. I will still continue, however, to examine the situation, and will write again Monday morning.

With many thanks and hearty sympathy,
Yours,
J. L. CHAMBERLAIN.

Hon. WM. T. DAVIS.

STATE OF RHODE ISLAND EXECUTIVE DEPARTMENT,
PROVIDENCE, Dec. 2, 1870.

GENTLEMEN, — Your cordial invitation to be present at the Two Hundred and Fiftieth Anniversary of the Landing of the Pilgrims at Plymouth, Dec. 21, 1870, is at hand. I regret to say, engagements will prevent my acceptance thereof.

Very respectfully,
Your obedient servant,
SETH PADELFORD.

Hon. WM. T. DAVIS, and others,
Plymouth, Mass.

OFFICE OF THE
"NORTH AMERICAN AND UNITED STATES GAZETTE,"
132 South Third Street,
PHILADELPHIA, Dec. 17, 1870.

MY DEAR SIR, — I have delayed my final answer to your several kind invitations, in the hopes that I might see my way clear to be with you on the occasion of your intended Celebration; but this I now fear will be impossible. In addition to the obstacles I have already mentioned, there are others, with the particulars of which I need not trouble you, that will effectually prevent my leaving here in time to reach Plymouth on the 21st inst. I regret this most sincerely.

If you should ever have occasion to come to Philadelphia, I trust you will give me the opportunity of showing you in person how fully I appreciate the courtesy you have shown in this matter; and in the mean while,

I am very truly yours,
MORTON McMICHAEL.

WM. T. DAVIS, Esq.

———◆———

PHILADELPHIA, Nov. 28th, 1870.

WM. T. DAVIS, and others,
    Committee of Arrangements.

GENTLEMEN, — Your invitation for Wednesday, December 21st, is received. I should take much pleasure in being present; but I fear that my engagements will prevent my leaving home at that time.

Thanking you most cordially for your kind invitation,

I am very truly yours,
JAY COOKE.

———◆———

ST. LOUIS, 30 Nov., 1870.

To the Committee of the Pilgrim Society of Plymouth, Mass.: —

Your invitation to the President of the New England Society of St. Louis, to meet you on the Two Hundred and Fiftieth Anniversary of the Landing of the Pilgrims, is recorded. I see you change your Celebration to the 21st of December. Throughout the West the 22d of December is looked upon as the proper day, and probably we shall have a celebration here on the 22d of December, which will prevent my attendance. Thanking you for the invitation, I would inquire the reason for changing the day, although we may not be able to conform to it.

Yours,

GEORGE PARTRIDGE, *President.*

NEW YORK, Dec. 4, 1870.

Hon. WM. T. DAVIS.

MY DEAR SIR, — I am chagrined to be unexpectedly called upon, by a parochial necessity, to recall my engagement to be present at the Pilgrim Celebration in Plymouth, on the 21st instant.

The marriage of one of the daughters of a very old and valued member of my society takes place on that day; and, as her pastor, I must give up every outside gratification to meet her natural desire for my nuptial benediction. I assure you that it is with special pain that I withdraw a promise from the fulfilment of which I had anticipated so much pleasure. Please regard me not as inconstant, but only as unfortunate in not being able to be in two agreeable places at the same time. One advantage will accrue to you: you will now have ten minutes to give to some other son of New England bursting with the desire to honor his Fathers at the expense of other people's patience.

With cordial regard and best wishes for the entire prosperity of your Two Hundred and Fiftieth Anniversary, I am your obliged and disappointed friend and servant,

HENRY W. BELLOWS.

BOSTON, Nov. 28th, 1870.

MY DEAR SIR, — I am very much obliged by your second note of the 22d, but unfortunately I am engaged also upon the "true day." But you will not miss my little rill of talk in your Niagara of eloquence.

Very truly yours,

GEORGE WILLIAM CURTIS.

Hon. WM. T. DAVIS.

---

52 WALL ST., NEW YORK.

DEAR SIR, — I have received your invitations to myself personally and to the President of the New England Society to attend the great Celebration of the Landing of the Pilgrims at Plymouth, on the

21st of December; and also your note of November 19th, promising to get me back to New York on the 22d. I feel very grateful for your kindness and that of the Committee, and wish it might be possible for me to come to Plymouth to attend the Celebration; but our Society in New York, ambitious to do its part on so noted an anniversary, has made preparations for an oration on the evening of the 21st, and a dinner on the evening of the 22d; and as Mr. Emerson has consented to come and deliver the oration, I feel in duty bound to be here and attend that. I must, therefore, with many thanks, decline your flattering invitation. I am happy to think, however, that our Society will be represented at your Celebration by some of its most honored members.

Your obedient servant,
JOSEPH H. CHOATE.

Hon. WM. T. DAVIS.

Will you please express to the Committee my thanks, and my very great regret at being compelled to decline their invitation.

NEW YORK TRIBUNE,
NEW YORK, Dec. 6th, 1870.

DEAR SIR, — I am very busy, and not very well, so I do not see how I can go to Plymouth.

Yours,
HORACE GREELEY.

ROSLYN, LONG ISLAND, Nov. 14th, 1870.

DEAR SIR, — I beg through you to thank the Committee of Arrangements, of which you are Chairman, for the invitation with which they have honored me, to be present at the Two Hundred and Fiftieth Anniversary of the landing of my ancestors, the Pilgrims, at Plymouth. Owing to various reasons, I must forego the pleasure of attending. I am, sir,

Very respectfully yours,
W. C. BRYANT.

W. T. DAVIS, Esq.

NEW YORK, Dec. 10th, 1870.

MY DEAR MR. DAVIS, — I have delayed answering your kind note of the 1st inst. until it should appear distinctly whether I might not be able to come on to Plymouth to your approaching Celebration, as I should be glad to do. I find, now, that it is out of the question for me to count upon being able to leave my professional engagements here for the proposed visit. I am sorry to lose Mr. Winthrop's oration, and the festivities of the occasion. I remember with much pleasure my former visit to Plymouth, and with my thanks for the remembrance of the Committee,

I am yours very truly,

WM. M. EVARTS.

W. T. DAVIS, Esq.

YALE COLLEGE, NEW HAVEN, CT.,
Nov. 23d, 1870.

WM. T. DAVIS, Esq., and others.

GENTLEMEN, — My engagements will probably be such that I shall be unable to spare the time to be present at the Anniversary of the Landing of the Pilgrims, as celebrated by the Pilgrim Society at Plymouth.

Accept my thanks for your hospitable invitation, and believe me, gentlemen, to be,

Yours gratefully,

THEODORE D. WOOLSEY.

BOSTON, Dec. 10th, 1870.

Hon. WM. T. DAVIS.

DEAR SIR, — I have the honor to acknowledge the courteous invitation of the Pilgrim Society to attend their Celebration at Plymouth, on Wednesday, the 21st inst., and to express my regret that I fear my engagements will not permit me to be present with them on so interesting an occasion.

Very respectfully,

E. R. HOAR.

BOSTON, Dec. 19th, 1870.

Hon. WILLIAM T. DAVIS.

DEAR SIR, — A case of bereavement, just announced to me in a telegram, will prevent my attendance at the commemoration festival to be held at Plymouth on Wednesday next; as, on the same day, in an adjacent State, and by the express desire of a highly esteemed friend, now happily released by death from excruciating suffering, and an incurable malady, I am to participate in the funeral rites demanded by the occasion. My absence, however, will not be missed in so large a company as will be gathered to pay their homage to the memory of the Pilgrim fathers and mothers of 1620; and my presence could add nothing to the significance of the occasion. The disappointment will be simply personal to myself. Nor should I think of stating to you the cause of my non-appearance, were it not for my acceptance of the invitation so kindly extended to me by yourself in behalf of the Committee of Arrangements.

It was in support of civil and religious liberty that the Pilgrims of the "Mayflower" encountered the most formidable dangers and made the most heroic sacrifices; their trust in God absolute, their reverence for his laws unbounded, their assertion of the rights of conscience fearless and uncompromising. However at variance with their spirit and object was the conduct of others who came to these shores afterward, and with whom they have been too often ignorantly and unjustly confounded, they made good their professions by their lives, and continued faithful to the end. In this they deserve to be applauded, and, better still, to be imitated. But no commemoration of their worth is deserving of record which is not inspired by a noble purpose to draw from their example incentives to higher aspirations, and a broader recognition of human rights than has yet been attained even in our land.

> "We, who are the seed
> Of buried creatures, if we turned and spat
> Upon our antecedents, we were vile.
> Bring violets, rather! If these had not walked
> Their furlong, could we hope to walk our mile?
> Therefore, bring violets! Yet, if we, self-balked,
> Stand still, a strewing violets all the while,
> These moved in vain of whom we've vainly talked.
> So rise up henceforth with a cheerful smile,
> And having reaped the violets, reap the corn,
> And having reaped and garnered, bring the plough,
> And draw new furrows 'neath the healthy morn,
> And plant the great Hereafter in this Now.
>   .   .   .   .   .
> O Dead, ye shall no longer cling to us
> With rigid hands of dessicating praise,
> And drag us backward by the garment thus,
> To stand and laud you in long-drawn virelays;
> We will not henceforth be oblivious
> Of our own lives because ye lived before,

> Nor of our acts because ye acted well.
> We thank you that ye first unlatched the door,
> But will not make it inaccessible
> By thankings on the thresholds any more.
> We hurry onward to extinguish hell
> With our fresh souls, our younger hope, and God's
> Maturity of purpose. Soon shall we
> Die also; and that then our periods
> Of life may round themselves to memory,
> As smoothly as on our graves the burial sods,
> We now must look to it to excel as ye,
> And bear our age as far, unlimited
> By the last mind mark; so to be invoked
> By future generations as their dead!"

Animated by considerations like these, we can alone be justified in observing the anniversary of the landing of the Pilgrim band at Plymouth Rock.

Yours for constant progress,

WM. LLOYD GARRISON.

P. S. — If I were present at your commemorative dinner, I could offer no sentiment more in accordance with my own mind, or more appropriate to the occasion, than is contained in the following lines by Lowell: —

"New occasions teach new duties; time makes ancient good uncouth;
They must upward still and onward, who would keep abreast of Truth.
Lo! before us gleam her camp-fires! we ourselves must Pilgrims be,
Launch our Mayflower, and steer boldly through the desperate winter sea,
Nor attempt the Future's portal with the Past's blood-rusted key."

BOSTON, Dec. 7, 1870.

I have delayed replying to your kind invitation till the present time in the hope that I might be able to accept it. But I find that my official engagements are such that I am very reluctantly compelled to forego that pleasure.

Yours very respectfully and truly,

R. A. CHAPMAN.

Hon. WM. T. DAVIS.

SALEM, Nov. 12, 1870.

Hon. WM. T. DAVIS,
    Chairman of Committee of Arrangements.

DEAR SIR, — I beg you to express to your Committee my thanks for the invitation you have conveyed to me. No occasion could have stronger attractions to me than the Celebration, on Dec. 21, 1870, at Plymouth, of the Landing of the Pilgrims. A very severe illness, from which I am appearing slowly to recover, will, at the best, leave me in a state that will forbid me leaving home, this winter, for any distance.

Please to express my regrets to your associates; and believe me, as ever,

Yours most affectionately,

CHARLES W. UPHAM.

WORCESTER, Dec. 1, 1870.

GENTLEMEN, — Your kind invitation to be present at the Celebration of the Landing of the Pilgrims has remained unanswered until now, in the hope that I might see my way to accept the honor. But I regret that the necessity of my being absent from the State at that time will compel me to forego the pleasure I otherwise should have in being with you on an occasion so laden with tender and solemn thoughts.

I remain, with profound respect,

Very truly your ob't serv't,

ALEX. H. BULLOCK.

BOSTON, Dec. 20, 1870.

MY DEAR SIR, — I received your invitation, and should have replied, but from its form supposed that a reply, unless in the affirmative, was not expected; and as I knew very well that I should be busy winding up matters preparatory to a session at the State House, I did not write.

I thank you very much for your kind remembrance of me, and regret that I cannot be present on an occasion which I know will be most enjoyable to all concerned.

Yours truly,

H. H. COOLEDGE.

BOSTON, Dec. 20th, 1870.

WM. T. DAVIS.

MY DEAR SIR, — I have to acknowledge the receipt of your recent and former note. With the pressure of professional engagements upon me, especially since my partner, Mr. Gaston, has been elected Mayor, and so rendered unable to attend to business, I have doubted whether I could be at Plymouth, and at this hour I cannot certainly say I can get away; but I hope to be with you, and make my excuses in person for my negligence. I hope I can get away. If not, accept my thanks for your kindness, and permit me to subscribe myself,

Yours very truly,
H. JEWELL.

HARVARD COLLEGE, CAMBRIDGE,
MASS., Dec. 8, 1870.

DEAR SIR, — I received, some time since, a kind invitation to attend the Pilgrim Celebration; and now Professor Goodwin has given me a message on the subject. My duties and engagements are so pressing that I find it quite impossible to undertake other labors or pleasures which are not near at hand. I am sorry that I must lose the pleasure of participating in this festival.

Very truly yours,
CHARLES W. ELIOT.

Hon. WM. T. DAVIS.

CAMBRIDGE, Nov. 19, 1870.

GENTLEMEN, — I have had the honor of receiving your invitation to be present at the Two Hundred and Fiftieth Anniversary of the Landing of the Pilgrims, and regret that it will not be in my power to accept it. Permit me to thank you for this mark of your regard, and believe me,

Yours faithfully,
HENRY W. LONGFELLOW.

Hon. WM. T. DAVIS, and others,
   Committee of Arrangements.

ATTORNEY GENERAL'S OFFICE,
BOSTON, Dec. 5th, 1870.

GENTLEMEN, — I am sorry to find that I shall not be able to attend the Celebration to which you have kindly invited me. With thanks for your courtesy,

I am very respectfully and truly yours,
CHARLES ALLEN.

Hon. WM. T. DAVIS, and others,
   Committee of Arrangements.

MIDDLEBORO', Dec. 14, 1870.

To WM. T. DAVIS, and others, Committee.

GENTLEMEN, — I very much regret that I shall be unable to comply with your kind invitation to be with you on the 21st inst.

I am very truly yours,

WM. H. WOOD.

BOSTON, Nov. 17, 1870.

MY DEAR SIR, — I thank you for your kind invitation to be at Plymouth on December 21st, but I am compelled to forego the pleasure I should take in being present, owing to a positive engagement for that evening in this city.

Very truly yours,

J. M. MANNING.

WESTON, Dec. 19, 1870.

Hon. WM. T. DAVIS, *et als.*

Duties which I do not feel at liberty to postpone will prevent my being present at the Celebration, next Wednesday, as I had before anticipated; though in heart and spirit I shall be with you in honoring the memory of the Pilgrim ancestors; who, with such toil and sacrifice, "kindled the light," to use Bradford's figure, "which hath shone to our whole Nation, as one small candle may light a thousand."

Yours sincerely,

E. H. SEARS.

CAMBRIDGE, Dec. 18, 1870.

GENTLEMEN, — I am greatly obliged by the honor of your invitation to the approaching Celebration of the Landing of the Pilgrims.

I count on being at Plymouth on that occasion; but, as it must depend on the weather and other circumstances, I respectfully request that I may not be considered in your arrangements.

I have the honor to be, Gentlemen,

Your obliged and humble servant,

JOHN G. PALFREY.

Hon. WM. T. DAVIS, and others,
    Committee of Arrangements.

NEW BEDFORD, Dec. 10th, 1870.

MY DEAR SIR, — I gratefully acknowledge the courtesy of the Committee having in charge the Two Hundred and Fiftieth Anniversary of the great Settlement of 1620, contained in their invitation to participate in the duties and pleasures of this commemoration.

I had hoped to see some way to snatch that day from business, and have delayed this acknowledgment for that cause. But I shall be obliged to spend the day in official duties in court, unless Judge Scudder should think that on such a day no court ought to sit in the Old Colony. For it would well suit the spirit of the day, if within the territorial limits of the Plymouth Colony all business should be suspended on that occasion, and the time be given up to the consideration of the grandest event in history.

Very truly yours,
GEO. MARSTON.

Hon. WM. T. DAVIS, Chairman, &c.

SALEM, December 17th, 1870.

GENTLEMEN, — Your communication, inviting me to be present at the Two Hundred and Fiftieth Anniversary of the Landing of the Pilgrims at Plymouth, has been received. I am grateful to you for the opportunity you have offered me to take part in the interesting ceremonies of the occasion; and I regret, more than I can express, that an engagement to speak in New York, which cannot be postponed, will prevent my enjoying the privilege you have extended to me. The suggestion of your chairman, Mr. Davis, that I should say something "in connection with the Essex settlement," has filled me with a sense of the obligation I am under to connect the locality in which I reside with a memorial service intended to perpetuate the memory of events in which Plymouth and Essex were mutually engaged in the early heroic days of our country. The story, I know, is familiar. Roger Conant, standing as a sentinel of Puritanism on the cliffs of Cape Ann, and John Endicott, obedient to the call of his great predecessor on this north shore, entered upon a service here which gave strength and courage to the Carvers and Bradfords of Plymouth, who had already given to the encircling shore of Massachusetts Bay the blessed reputation of a protecting arm for high religious purpose, a firm and abiding faith, a stern conscience, and the right of all men to enter God's holy church and share in the honors and responsibilities of a Christian State.

In this great work, it was given to Plymouth, indeed, to lead the way. The path which her Pilgrims trod from England to Leyden, from Leyden to Delft-Haven and Southampton, and thence to the shores of America, will be traced in all coming time, with fervid interest, by every lover of the divine power in man. To all the brave and thoughtful, the names of Robinson and Bradford and Carver will always be dear; and there will be none to share with them the immortal honor of having inspired an empire of freedom and faith. But we, who occupy this soil upon which John Endicott, "a fit instrument to begin this wilderness work," and "the excellent and truly Catholic" Francis Higginson, first trod, rejoice over Plymouth, as children in the honor and greatness of their father, and claim for ourselves a share in the great inheritance. We love to remember the mission of the good physician of Plymouth, who, when our ancestors on the Naumkeag side were broken down by disease, crossed the Bay and landed here on his errand of mercy. We listen to the religious discussion between this messenger of kindness and Governor Endicott, upon predestination, " fixed fate, free will, and foreknowledge absolute;" upon the primitive simplicity of Christianity; upon the aggressions and encroachments of Episcopacy; and perhaps upon that great Puritan Commonwealth just rising into existence, and confirming by the hardships of its youth those qualities which have made its manhood so strong and triumphant. We recall, as a mutual possession for Essex and Plymouth, the correspondence which then commenced between Governor Endicott and Governor Bradford, — the interchanging thought of two giant minds laden with solemn duties and responsibilities for their own generation and for all after time. And by the side of Rose Standish, the morning and the evening star of the Pilgrims, we place Arbella Johnson, the "Flower of Lincoln," the delicious ornament of our gloomy Naumkeag settlement, whose life was the light, and whose death was the shadow, which first fell upon our colony;[17] and of each of whom we may say, —

> "The saintly faith that bore her soul
> Where clouds no more are known,
> Save by the fruits their tear-drops helped
> To ripen round the throne, —
> Yes, that pure love, that hallowed faith,
> Have reared above her clay
> Such monument and epitaph
> As may not wear away."

To us the memory of these early associations of our ancestors, united in a great cause, is peculiarly sacred; and I am sure that I do but utter the sentiment of every descendant of the heroic settlers of Naumkeag, and the feelings of all our citizens, when I express the gratitude we feel that the " Essex settlement " may share the renown which has gathered around the stern and devoted purpose of the Plymouth Colony. For the courtesy extended to them and to myself, in the fraternal suggestions accompanying your invitation, allow me to express my sincere and grateful acknowledgments, and I doubt not theirs.

Respectfully and truly yours,
GEO. B. LORING.

Hon. WM. T. DAVIS, WM. H. WHITMAN, Esq.,
    Hon. CHAS. G. DAVIS, and others, Committee, Plymouth.

AMESBURY, 12th mo. 17th, 1870.

Hon. W. T. DAVIS, and others, Committee.

GENTLEMEN, — I regret that it is impossible for me to accept your invitation to attend the Celebration of the Two Hundred and Fiftieth Anniversary of the Landing of the Pilgrims at Plymouth. No one can appreciate more highly than myself the noble qualities of the men and women of the "Mayflower." It is not of them that I, a descendant of the sect called "Quakers," have reason to complain in the matter of persecution. A generation which came after them, with less piety and more bigotry, is especially responsible for the little unpleasantness referred to; and the sufferers from it scarcely need any present championship. They certainly did not wait altogether for the revenges of posterity. If they lost their ears, it is satisfactory to remember that they made those of their mutilators tingle with a rhetoric more sharp than polite.

A worthy New England deacon once described a brother in the church as a very good man God-ward, but rather hard man-ward. It cannot be denied that some very satisfactory steps have been taken in the latter direction, at least since the days of the Pilgrims. Our age is tolerant of creed and dogma, broader in its sympathies, more keenly sensitive to temporal need; and, practically recognizing the brotherhood of the race, wherever a cry of suffering is heard its response is quick and generous. It has abolished slavery, and is lifting women from world-old degradation to equality with man before the law. Our criminal codes no longer embody the maxim of barbarism, "an eye for an eye and a tooth for a tooth," but have regard not only to the safety of the community, but to the reform and well-being of the criminal. All the more, however, for this amiable tenderness do we need the counterpoise of a strong sense of justice. With our sympathy for the wrong-doer, we need the old Puritan and Quaker hatred of wrong-doing; with our just tolerance of men and opinions, a righteous abhorrence of sin. All the more for the sweet humanities and Christian liberalism which, in drawing men nearer to each other, are increasing the sum of social influences for good or evil, we need the bracing atmosphere, healthful if austere, of the old moralities. Individual and social duties are quite as imperative now as when they were minutely specified in statute-books and enforced by penalties no longer admissible. It is well that stocks, whipping-post, and ducking-stool are now only matters of tradition; but the honest reprobation of vice and crime which they symbolized should by no means perish with them. The true life of a nation is in its personal morality, and no excellence of constitution and laws can avail much if the people lack purity and integrity. Culture, art, refinement, care for our own comfort and that of others, are well; but truth, honor, reverence, and fidelity to duty, are indispensable.

The Pilgrims were right in affirming the paramount authority of the law of God. If they erred in seeking that authoritative law, and passed over the Sermon on the Mount for the stern Hebraisms of Moses; if they hesitated in view of the largeness of Christian liberty; if they seemed unwilling to accept the sweetness and light of the Good Tidings, — let us not forget that it was the mistake of men who feared more than they dared to hope; whose estimate of the exceeding sinfulness of sin caused them to dwell upon God's vengeance rather than His compassion; and whose dread of evil was so great that, in shutting their hearts against it, they sometimes shut out the good. It is well for us if we have learned to listen to the sweet persuasion of the Beatitudes, but there are crises in all lives which require also the emphatic "Thou shalt not" of the Decalogue which the Founders wrote on the gate-posts of their Commonwealth.

Let us then be thankful for the assurance which the last few years have afforded us that

> "The Pilgrim spirit is not dead,
> But walks in noon's broad light."

We have seen it in the faith and trust which no circumstances could shake; in heroic self-sacrifice, in entire consecration to duty. The Fathers have lived in their sons. Have we not all known the Winthrops and Brewsters, the Saltonstalls and Sewalls, — of the old time in gubernatorial chairs, in legislative halls, — around winter camp-fires, in the slow martyrdoms of prison and hospital? The great struggle through which we have passed has taught us how much we owe to the men and women of the Plymouth Colony, — the noblest ancestry that ever a people looked back to with love and reverence. Honor, then, to the Pilgrims! Let their memory be green for ever!

Truly your friend,
JOHN G. WHITTIER.

NOTES.

1.—PAGE 7.

Extract from the Records of the Pilgrim Society, Plymouth, Mass.

SATURDAY, DECEMBER 15th, 1849.

Voted, That a Committee be appointed, consisting of James Savage, Charles H. Warren, Nathaniel B. Shurtleff, of Boston, and Timothy Gordon and Abraham Jackson, of Plymouth, to consider the expediency of celebrating in future the Landing of the Pilgrims, on the twenty-first day of December, instead of the twenty-second, and that said Committee report at the next regular meeting, on the last Monday of May next.

MONDAY, MAY 27th, 1850.

At this meeting, the Committee appointed in December last, to consider the expediency of altering the day of celebrating the Landing of the Pilgrims, presented a full and able Report on the subject, which, after a general discussion of the same, was unanimously accepted, and ordered to be printed.

Voted, That this Society will hereafter regard the *twenty-first* day of December, as the true anniversary of the Landing of the Pilgrims.

A true copy from the Records of the Pilgrim Society.

WILLIAM S. RUSSELL, *Recording Secretary.*

THE Committee of the Pilgrim Society, appointed, at the meeting in December last, " to consider the expediency of celebrating in future the Landing of the Pilgrims, on the twenty-first day of December, instead of the twenty-second," having duly considered the subject, submit the following as their Report : —

That the happy Monday, on which our fathers came, for the first time, on shore at Plymouth from the shallop, wherein they had "circulated the Bay" between Cape Cod and this harbor, and, having on Friday preceding got to anchor under the lee of Clark's Island, had there quietly spent the Sunday, after return of thanks to God on Saturday for deliverance in their great peril from breaking the rudder and the mast, and losing the sail — this Monday when they "marched into the land, saw the corn fields, and running brooks, judged the place fit for habitation, and returned to the ship," as Bradford, who was of the exploring party, assures us, " with the discovery to their great comfort," is the very day that all of us desire to honor as the birth day of Christian freedom and true civilization in New England.

Reverence for progenitors, as well as self-respect, forbids us to permit any mixture of fiction with the great truths of their story. By any such artifice it can never be brightened; as it will not be darkened, we are confident, either by disreputable facts or evil surmises. When paying our ancestors the debt of gratitude, we should rather exclude, than encourage, such doubtful traditions, as the ignorant are wont to heap on important events. Who first landed on the rock? was once an idle inquiry, thought to be met by the claims of Mary Chilton, till an equal competitor was found in John Alden;— as if each pretence were not childish;— as if we did not know, that Alden was not one of the twelve that first came in the shallop, that no woman was within many miles of this spot for several days, and that Mary Chilton, especially, was occupied in attendance on her dying father, who lived but two days after the little expedition left Cape Cod harbor. Every incident of the doing and suffering of our fathers near that time should be fresh in our memories, as if it had occurred last week; and to preserve exactness of date, most agreeable is the coincidence of this happy landing with the recurrence, almost to an hour precisely, of the Winter solstice.

That memorable Monday was 21st December, according to the Almanacs then used by the larger part of the Christian world, to which the residue of us, except adherents to the Greek platform of the church, have since conformed; but in the Almanac of our fathers, or old style, that day was the 11th December, 1620. However there can be no doubt about an identical day, let nominal dates be ever so diverse, because the week days will be the same, whether old or new style be employed. Truth spread slowly in this direction. Since the church of Rome reformed the Calendar, on advice of the ablest mathematicians of Europe, forty years had not run to the coming of the Pilgrims; and the prejudice, not the wisdom, of our King, Lords, and Commons, in Parliament assembled, continued to reject the improvement one hundred and thirty years longer. Yet it was not ignorance, but more blame-worthy cause, that made the numbering of days in the month so different, between England and other nations. The practise of inoculation for the small pox we borrowed from the Turks, many years before our repugnance to the Catholic church would receive from its supporters needful correction of an arithmetical falsehood in our Almanac.

A simple illustration may be agreeable to those who have not either leisure to follow a brief demonstration, or memory to preserve naked numbers. Capt. Allerton, when he went home to England in the Autumn of 1626, we may suppose, crossed the channel in December, to meet the Huguenot brethren in France. This was the first year since his landing at Plymouth, in which the days of the month and days of the week coincided with those of 1620; and on Saturday, 9th, by his English reckoning, he must have remembered the anchorage under Clark's Island;— the sacred rest of Sunday, the 10th;— and the glad bounding upon land of Monday, the 11th. Did he not require his brethren in the faith to rejoice with him on the anniversary of religious freedom, established at Plymouth, for the first time beneath the sun, six years before? Did he ask them to mark the day in their Almanacs for observation in years to come? Did they not forthwith agree, that *this* day, the 21st, in theirs, but 11th in Allerton's count, must forever be honored? Their Calendar being already reformed, the third Monday of December, 1620, or 1626, being the 21st day of the month, that number in the line of this month would indicate the exact day in succeeding years of the same or any following century, 1720, 1820, or 1920; while the unreformed style, counting, as the Huguenots did not, 1700 for a leap year, and so twenty-nine days in February, the just equivalent of 11th December, 1699, by which it should be shown, that a year was gone, must of course be the 10th instead of 11th. The very year's day is the one we would reverence. It is not the gathering crowds of 22d of December, 1769, the earliest public observance, that we would exemplify; but only show our admiration for the landing upon Plymouth rock of the blessed few, at the Winter solstice of 1620, on the day which in the reformed Almanac at that time, and since September, 1752, in those of England and of us, who claim all the rights and more than the benefits of Englishmen, has been, and for many thousand years to come will be, truly noted as the twenty-first day of December.

The necessity of adding ten, eleven, or twelve, or more days to the number of the day of the month, in old style, depends not on the time when we inquire about the event to which this addition shall be applied, but to the century when that event occurred. In the sixth century the running of erroneous computation had made only one day's deviation; but this uniform mistake in reckoning of a few minutes and seconds in the length of a year had swelled, in the seventeenth century, when Plymouth was settled by our fathers, to ten days. Had this been a century later, the 11th of December, 1720, it would require eleven days for making our old style, then the legal one, concur with the reformed style, because 1700 was counted a leap year by us, but not by the most of the Christians who had before got upon the right track. In this nineteenth century twelve days must be added, yet, of course, only to occurrences of this century. By the Calendar of the Greek church, the day of the battle of Waterloo is marked on 6th of June, which in 1815 was a Sunday; and that Sunday of slaughter is, in all the West of Europe, noted as the 18th of that month.

In the first half of the last century, before the change of supputation was made by law, memorable events, as the birth of Franklin, of Washington, of King George III., of the capture of Louisburg, may have been observed by parties more or less numerous; but this observation, we may, on a moment's reflection, be sure, was in each case held, or should have been, on a day nominally eleven days later, after the 2d of September, 1752,— because between the second and fourteenth of that month there was no day in the Almanac. THE MONTH HAD BUT NINETEEN DAYS. A date of 3d, or 4th, or 5th of September, 1751, at the end of one year from it, was to be found only as fourteenth, fifteenth, or sixteenth, severally. Statute provision was simple enough, relative to rents, interest and such things; but common sense was left to regulate less important matters. The last day of old style, under our law, being Wednesday, 2d of September, the next day would be Thursday, whether the law was obeyed, requiring it to be called 14th — or perverse fanaticism called it the 3d. We know, that a person born on the 14th of September, 1752, will be ninety-eight years old on 14th of September next. Why then shall one born *one day earlier* be called ninety-eight, (because his birth-day was Wednesday 2d September, 1752.) eleven days before the just fulfilment of his last year? Between one year and its successor, settlement of this difference is easy enough to the humblest capacity. The matter is determined by the exact, *natural* day, week, or year. Our common year consists of fifty-two weeks and one day; a leap year, of fifty-two weeks and two days. A child born on Monday, 31st August, 1752, could not be a year old on 31st August, 1753, because he had lived only fifty weeks and four days; for another, born the next Monday, 18th September was his birthday, inasmuch as there was no 7th in that month, eleven days being suppressed, or cancelled. On 13th September, 1753, the child must be reckoned only one year old, if born on 2d September of the former year; but one born 2d September, 1652, would fill his one hundred and one years on 12th September, 1753, because (since the century when he was born was only *ten*, not *eleven*, days behind true reckoning) he was really one hundred years old on 1st September, 1752. He did not wait for the eighteenth century to demand eleven days, for ten was enough, of addition to his date; but paid the difference of fare, one day, so to speak, in passing through the gate of 1700, which was reckoned a leap year in old style, but not in the new, and better, computation of these venerable divisions of time.

But, though the quantity of correction must vary with the length of time in which the error has been growing, when the correction is once applied, it is done forever. Had our style been changed in the *eighth* century, three days would have been sufficient to add; while eleven were found necessary by our law-makers in the *last;* and in the *present,* our Russian correspondents are twelve days behind us. We make no more addition since September, 1752; nor did the continental arithmeticians to their *less* contribution, having earlier adjusted their reckoning. Yet it is sometimes heedlessly spoken of as proper to add twelve days, which is indeed renewing the mistake, and consecrating the ignorance by which the chronology was corrupted before.

In the celebration eighty years ago, this error of one day is easily accounted for. We may well presume, that one or more of our genial Old Colony club, who honored forefathers' day with public celebration, for the first time, in 1769, had served in the memorable expedition of 1745, against Cape Breton, and had for several previous years glorified, in succession, the 16th of June, as the day of surrender of Louisburg. To that numeral in the Almanac they adhered, of course, for seven years; but they had for the next seventeen years been compelled to denote the exact day of any interesting occurrence in that century by addition of eleven days to its prior standing, and of course reached the 27th of June as their true anniversary. Such enumeration was inadvertently applied, instead of the scrupulously exact one, to the blessed day of the landing, though that event was one hundred and forty-nine years before the celebration, and so much nearer to the starting place of the perversity.

Of these glorious mile-stones of memory the consecrations have, in our day, been numerous; yet the false assumption of a day for that ceremony has been too frequent. In honor of the landing of Endicot, at Salem, on 6th September, 1628, the Essex Historical Society took in 1825 the same nominal 6th as the equivalent, — an error to be explained, if not justified, by fondness felt for the mere number, yet which would have been avoided, if any had inquired what day was observed in 1752, when the Statute of 24 George II., 1751, said, there should be *no* 6th. For the solemn pomp of the observation of the two hundredth anniversary of the same happy occurrence, three years later, a wrong day was again assumed. Instead of 16th, as it ought to have been, unhappily they took the

18th, which appears, in one sense, a worse error than the former, inasmuch as it must be more blamable to outrun the truth than to fall behind it. Confident we may be, at least, that when September, 1928 comes, the citizens of Salem will not feel bound to celebrate the 19th day of the month. Of this mistake the cause may, *then*, be recollected. Being asked, a few days before the festival, what is the difference between old and new style, the greatest mathematician of our country gave answer, according to the truth, in the open street, without more conference, in his prompt manner, *twelve days;* — yet Dr. Bowditch afterwards said, when it was too late, the question should have been, — what *was* the difference two hundred years ago?

At the celebration in Charlestown, of the landing of Gov. Winthrop, in 1630, 17th June, part of the Salem error was followed, and the 28th of June, 1830, stood for its representative. By this repetition of mistake, within so brief space, attention to the subject was attracted; and when the two hundred years from the naming of Boston were elapsed, the late Judge Davis, and others, took much interest in showing that the 7th of September, 1630, found its true equivalent in the day, 17th September, 1830, selected for its solemn commemoration. If we feel, that we have gone long enough in the wrong path, we may see by this illustration, that it is not too late to get upon the right. Another occasion for scrutiny into exact concurrence of days, after so many revolutions in the sky, is recollected but a short time since. When the Massachusetts Historical Society resolved to honor the second centennial of the confederation of the four New England Colonies, and appointed the late John Quincy Adams to deliver an Address upon the importance of that act of 19th of May, 1643, his first thought, perhaps from association with long residence in Russia, was of the necessity for twelve days required by transference of that date into our computation. But by looking forward on the line of procession of the Greek church, in which the error increases by regular lapse of time, he soon perceived that the same cause of departure from the truth having been at work since the vernal equinox of A. D. 325, shortly before the Council of Nice met, and having worked equally, would show different lengths of deviation in different times; and felt that the path behind could be made straight by the same rule which alone must bring to our standard the vexatious chronology of the Eastern patriarch. In that foreign land every letter-writer, as he uses the Old style, prays for its correction, not so much because our 13th of April is their All-fool's day at St. Petersburg, as because the perpetuity of their reckoning in every four hundred years three days short will, in the year of grace 12000, carry the seasons one quarter round, and so the spring will be well advanced on 21st of December. Let the perversity be continued, another equal term, and the Almanac of the Czar shall dignify as the Winter solstice, the same day that his neighbors of Sweden and Denmark celebrate as having the longest sunlight of the year.

In the present question, it may seem, that no important consequences will come of our following the right counting, when we have so long been accustomed to a different one; yet surely we ought not to be censured for feeling too proud to go wrong, when we know the path is wrong. As the exact equivalent of that 11th of December, 1620, in our English Almanac, was the 21st of December in that of France, and we have since admitted our error, and the correctness of the other reckoning, by solemn act of legislation, why should we celebrate a day later for that of our fathers' landing? The truth should be good enough for us; and that is the only reason for preference of one to another. When by habit the right day has become the day of reverence, it will be wondered, why the wrong was so often observed. Next year, indeed, the true anniversary falling on Sunday, it may be more conformable to New England principles, to celebrate the following, or 22d day of the month; but we presume nobody would desire a further carrying forward of the festival to the 23d. though our elder brothers of the Old Colony club, before the Revolution, once did to the 24th.

Your Committee conclude their Report, which may, indeed, seem tiresome from its repetition of the matter with so slight variations as this popular form made unavoidable, by recommendation to the Society of the following Order:—

That the celebration in future of the Landing of the Pilgrims at Plymouth be held on the *twenty-first* day of December; but when that day falls on Sunday, then to be held on the twenty-second.

Respectfully submitted.

JAS. SAVAGE,
C. H. WARREN,
NATHL. B. SHURTLEFF,
ABRAHAM JACKSON,
TIMOTHY GORDON.

2. — PAGE 7.

Hon. ROBERT C. WINTHROP, born in Boston, is son of Thomas Lindall Winthrop, Lieutenant-Governor of Massachusetts from 1826 to 1832, who was the son of John Still Winthrop, of New

London, who was son of John, a member of the Council of Connecticut, and of the Royal Society, who was son of Wait Still Winthrop, Chief Justice of the Superior Court of Massachusetts, who was son of John, Governor of Connecticut, who was son of John, Governor of Massachusetts, who was son of Adam, of London, afterwards Lord of the Manor at Groton, in Suffolk County, England, and died 1623, who was son of Adam, of Groton, also Lord of the Manor, died 1562, who was son of Adam, who lived in 1498 at Lavenham. The second and third Adam, the father and grandfather of Governor Winthrop, were buried in the family tomb now bearing the family name and arms, in the church-yard of Groton Church, in England. The town of Groton in Connecticut received its name from the Winthrops, in honor of their old family residence. The name of Still, found in the Winthrop family, is derived from the first wife of Adam, the father of John, of Massachusetts, who was Alice Still, sister of Dr. John Still, Master of Trinity and Vice-Chancellor of the University of Cambridge, and Bishop of Bath and Wells. Governor John Winthrop, of Massachusetts, was born at Edwardston, near the family seat at Groton, Jan. 12, 1587 (old style), arrived at Salem, June 12, 1630, and died in Boston, March 26, 1649.

3. — PAGE 8.

Under the direction of the Finance Committee, a guarantee fund was raised by subscription, amounting to sixteen hundred dollars, to defray such expenses of the Celebration as the receipts from the sale of dinner and ball tickets might fail to meet.

4. — PAGE 17.

The ode of Hon. JOHN DAVIS is here printed as revised and corrected by its author about fifty years after it was written. What is now the third verse was not included in the original; what is now the sixth verse was originally the fifth, and written as follows: —

> Columbia, child of Heaven!
> The best of blessings given
> Rest on thy head;
> Beneath thy peaceful skies,
> While prosperous tides arise,
> Here turn thy grateful eyes,
> Revere the dead.

In the original, the first verse was repeated at the end.

5.—Page 23.

MUSIC

Composed by C. A. White, for the Hymn written by Wm. T. Davis.

6. — Page 115.

BILL OF FARE.

———

Soup.   Succotash.

Boiled.

Chicken (with Pork).   Mutton (Caper Sauce).
Cold Pressed Corned Beef.   Cold Beef Tongue.

Entrées.

Escalloped Oysters.   Chicken Salad.

Relishes.

Worcestershire Sauce.   Walnut Ketchup.
Leicestershire Sauce.   Mushroom Ketchup.
India Soy.   Cauliflower.
London Club Sauce.   Mixed Pickles.

Roast.

Lamb.   Sirloin Beef.   Turkey.   Goose.
Chicken.   Sugar-cured Ham.   Mutton.

Vegetables.

Potatoes.   Beets.   Squash.   Celery.
Turnips.   Cranberries.   Onions.

Pastry.

Plum Pudding, (Wine Sauce).   Apple Pie.
Plain, Frosted, and Fruit Cake.   Washington Pie.
Maccaroni and Cocoa Cakes.   Squash Pie.
Chess Cake.   Pumpkin Pie.

Dessert.

Vanilla Ice Cream.   Strawberry Ice Cream.
Apples.   Raisins.   Assorted Nuts.
Assorted Confectionery.
Coffee.   Tea.

———

7. — Page 115.

"In 1623 the Colony of Plymouth was reduced at one time to one pint of corn, which, when divided, gave five grains to each person."

8. — PAGE 117.

It is well known that not one of the Pilgrims returned in the "May-Flower." In connection with this vessel, it is proper here to say that there is not a particle of evidence to authorize or justify the loose statement, sometimes made, that she was engaged in the slave trade after her return to England. All that is known of this famous vessel is, that, at different times, she hailed from London, Yarmouth, and Southampton, and not only brought the Pilgrims to Plymouth, but was one of the four vessels which transported Mr. HIGGINSON and his company to Salem in 1629, and one of the fleet which conveyed to New England, in 1630, John WINTHROP and the early settlers of the Massachusetts Colony.

9. — PAGE 125.

October 25, 1632, Governor WINTHROP, with Mr. WILSON, pastor of Boston, was carried by Mr. PIERCE, of the ship "Lyon," in his shallop, to Weymouth, which, under the aboriginal name of Wessaguscus, Wessaguscussett, Wessagussett, Wichaguscussett, or Wessagusquassett, had been settled in 1622, by a small colony under THOMAS WESTON, which was broken up the following year. The next morning the party journeyed on foot, pursuing the Indian trail, over very much the route of the present Plymouth and Boston road. They passed what was then and is now called Hewes' Cross, at Curtis' Mill, on the third herring brook on the boundary line between South Scituate and Hanover, named after JOHN HEWES, one of the earliest settlers of Scituate, and crossed the Indian Head branch of North River at a ford about a mile above the bridge on the Boston road, which WINTHROP called Luddam's Ford, after his guide, who carried him on his back across the river. This place is now known by the name of Ludden's Ford; and DEANE, in his History of Scituate, says he has no doubt that the guide was JAMES LUDDEN, one of the early settlers of Weymouth. Their route from the North River was through Pembroke and Kingston. See Savage's Winthrop, vol. i. p. 91 — Barry — First Period — p. 198; and Deane's Scituate, pages 160 and 162.

10. — PAGE 127.

JOHN ENDICOTT was born in Dorchester, England, in the year 1588. He sailed from Weymouth in the ship "Abigail," June 20,

1628, and arrived at Naumkeag, the place of destination, on the 6th of September following. He died in Boston, March 15, 1665. FRANCIS HIGGINSON had been a non-conformist clergyman of the Church of England. Of Jesus College and St. John's, Cambridge, and subsequently rector of a church at Leicester, he had been deprived of his benefice for non-conformity. He arrived at Naumkeag June 30, 1629, was chosen teacher soon after his arrival, and died in 1630.

11. — PAGE 127.

April 12, 1632, Governor WINTHROP received letters from Plymouth, stating that Capt. STANDISH, having a fight with the Indians at Sowamsett, needed powder, an article of which Plymouth Colony was then destitute. The Governor sent the messenger back with as much as he could carry, — to wit, twenty-seven pounds. In August following, THOMAS DUDLEY, Deputy-Governor of Massachusetts, made public charges against Governor WINTHROP, the second of which was that he had lent powder to Plymouth Colony without authority. To this charge the Governor answered, "It was of his own powder, and upon their urgent distress, their own powder proving naught, when they were to send to the rescue of their men at Sowamsett."

12. — PAGE 130.

The Compact signed in the cabin of the May-Flower in Cape Cod Harbor.

In the name of God, Amen. We whose names are underwritten, the loyal subjects of our dread sovereign lord, King James, by the grace of God, of Great Britain, France, and Ireland King, defender of the faith, etc., having undertaken, for the glory of God, and advancement of the Christian faith, and honor of our King and country, a voyage to plant the first colony on the northern parts of Virginia, do, by these presents, solemnly and mutually in the presence of God and one of another, covenant and combine ourselves together into a civil body politic, for our better ordering and preservation, and furtherance of the ends aforesaid; and by virtue hereof do enact constitute and frame such just and equal laws, ordinances, acts, constitutions, and offices, from time to time, as shall be thought most meet and convenient for the general good of the Colony; unto which we promise all due submission and obedience. In witness whereof we have hereunder subscribed our names, at Cape Cod, the 11th of November in the year of our sovereign lord, King James, of England, France and Ireland the eighteenth, and of Scotland the fifty-fourth, anno Domini 1620.

Mr. John Carver	8	John Alden		1
William Bradford	2	Mr. Samuel Fuller		2
Mr. Edward Winslow	5	,, Christopher Martin		4
,, William Brewster	6	,, William Mullins		5
,, Isaac Allerton	6	,, William White		5
Capt. Miles Standish	2	,, Richard Warren		1
John Howland		John Goodman		1
Mr. Stephen Hopkins	8	Degory Priest		1
Edward Tilly	4	Thomas Williams		1
John Tilly	3	Gilbert Winslow		1
Francis Cook	2	Edmund Margeson		1
Thomas Rogers	2	Peter Brown		1
Thomas Tinker	3	Richard Britterige		1
John Ridgdale	2	George Soule		
Edward Fuller	3	Richard Clarke		1
John Turner	3	Richard Gardener		1
Francis Eaton	3	John Allerton		1
James Chilton	3	Thomas English		1
John Crackston	2	Edward Dotey		
John Billington	4	Edward Leister		
Moses Fletcher	1			

This list of names, with their titles, is taken from Governor BRADFORD's manuscript. This accounts, probably, for the omission of the title of "Mr." to his name. The figures opposite each name designate the number in each family; and the four persons whose names have no numbers against them are included in the families of some of the others.

13. — PAGE 141.

The words, "treasures hid in the sand," quoted from the 19th verse of chapter xxxiii. of Deuteronomy, and often used in allusion to the Pilgrims, sometimes has reference to the abundance of shell-fish with which they were supplied, and sometimes to the corn which the Indians had buried in the sand, some of which was discovered by the exploring party sent out from Provincetown on Wednesday, the 15th of November, 1620, "under the conduct of Capt. MILES STANDISH, unto whom was adjoined, for counsel and advice, WILLIAM BRADFORD, STEPHEN HOPKINS, and EDWARD TILLEY."

14. — PAGE 142.

General JOHN WINSLOW was the great-grandson of Governor EDWARD WINSLOW. He was, in 1740, a captain in the expedition to Cuba, and was engaged in the enterprises against Crown Point and Nova Scotia, and to the Kennebec, in the two French wars. His agency in the removal of the Acadians from Nova Scotia, in 1755, is well known, at which time he was a half-pay captain in the British army and a major-general in the militia. In this affair, WINSLOW acted under written instructions from Lieutenant-Governor CHARLES LAWRENCE, of Nova Scotia, and cannot fairly be charged with inhumanity. In 1756 he commanded eight thousand New England men against Montcalm, and in 1762 was appointed commissioner with WILLIAM BRATTLE and JAMES OTIS to determine the easterly boundary line. He died at Hingham, in 1774, aged seventy-one. See Sabine's Loyalists of the Revolution, vol. ii. p. 439.

15. — PAGE 158.

Plymouth is generally supposed to have been named by the Pilgrims after Plymouth in England, which was the last place from which the "May-Flower" sailed. It is stated by Palfrey, in his History of New England, vol. i. p. 94, that JOHN SMITH, on his return to England from his expedition, in 1614, sent a copy of a map of the New England Coast, from near the mouth of the Penobscot to Cape Cod, to Prince Charles, afterwards Charles the First, who, at his solicitation, gave names, principally of English towns, to some thirty points upon the coast. The names of Plymouth, Cape Ann, and Charles River, have permanently adhered to the places they were selected by the Prince to designate.

16. — PAGE 162.

EDWARD WINSLOW, Jr., nephew of General JOHN WINSLOW, graduated at Harvard University in 1765. In 1774 he was one of the two clerks of the Court of General Sessions of the Peace and Court of Common Pleas for Plymouth County. In 1775 he joined the Royal Army at Boston, and became a colonel. In 1778 he was proscribed and banished, and in 1782 was Muster-Master-General of the Loyalist forces. After the war, he settled in New Brunswick, and was a member of the first Council in that Colony, Surrogate-General, Judge of the Supreme Court, and finally Administrator of the Government. He died at Frederickton, in 1815, aged seventy years. He resided in the house in North Street, in Plymouth, called the Winslow House, with his father Edward Winslow, who built it. Edward Winslow, the father, graduated at Cambridge in 1736, was one of the clerks of the Court, Register of Probate, and Collector of the Port of Plymouth. He left the country with his family in 1776, and went to Halifax, Nova Scotia, where he died in 1784, aged seventy-two years. See Sabine's Loyalists of the Revolution, vol. ii. p. 445.

17. — PAGE 186.

The name of Lady ARBELLA JOHNSON has been incorrectly spelled by even such writers as Neal, Hutchinson, and Trumbull, by whom it was called *Arabella*. She was the daughter of Thomas, third Earl of Lincoln, who was descended from a family that came into England with William the Conqueror. Her brother, Theophilus, became the fourth Earl on the death of his father, January 15, 1619. She married Isaac Johnson, and came to Salem with her husband, in company with Governor WINTHROP, in the "Eagle," of three hundred and fifty tons, carrying twenty-eight guns and fifty men, whose name had been changed to "Arbella," in compliment to her. She arrived on the 12th of June, and coming, as Hubbard says, "from a paradise of plenty and pleasure, which she enjoyed in the family of a noble earldom, into a wilderness of wants," survived her arrival only a month. Her husband, Isaac Johnson, was the richest man of the colony. According to Sewall, he died Sept. 30, 1630, in Boston, and, at his own request, was buried in what is now King's Chapel burial-ground. The people manifested their respect for his memory by ordering their bodies to be buried near him; and in this way the spot became a burial-ground, and has so continued to this day. Other writers claim that he died in Charlestown, and doubt the authenticity of the tradition relating to his burial. See Eliot's Biographical Dictionary, p. 281; and Young's Chronicles of Massachusetts, p. 218.

HYMN.

Written by Capt. NATHANIEL SPOONER, of Plymouth.

GREAT GOD of all! in humble, grateful prayer
    We come before Thee now on bended knee,
And thank Thee that Thou didst our Fathers spare
    From the wild dangers of a wintry sea.

We thank Thee that, when dangers greater far
    Encompassed them, that brave hearts might appall,
Thou didst support them, and didst let the Star
    Of Hope shine on their hearts and strengthen all.

And we, their children, on this joyous day,
    No longer peril-driven or tempest-tossed,
Approach Thy throne in thankfulness, and pray
    Our Fathers' bright examples be not lost.

May we, like them, have strength and courage given;
    Bear bravely up, e'en though we feel the rod;
Know that a life well spent leads on to heaven,
    And *duties'* paths are but the paths to God.

Cambridge: Press of John Wilson and Son.

www.ingramcontent.com/pod-product-compliance
Lightning Source LLC
Chambersburg PA
CBHW021728220426
43662CB00008B/749